Cult Leaders

Other Books in the History Makers Series:

History MAKERS

Cult Leaders

By Karen Burns Kellaher

Lucent Books
P.O. Box 289011, San Diego, CA 92198-9011

*To my parents, for teaching me
to meet the world with open eyes and
an open mind*

Library of Congress Cataloging-in-Publication Data

Kellaher, Karen Burns, 1969–
    Cult leaders / by Karen Burns Kellaher.
        p. cm.—(History makers)
    Includes bibliographical references and index.
    Summary: Profiles the lives and unusual teachings of six charismatic
cult leaders: Mother Ann Lee, Father Divine, L. Ron Hubbard,
Sun Myung Moon, Jim Jones, and David Koresh.
    ISBN 1–56006–593–1 (lib. bdg. : alk. paper)
    1. Religious biography—United States—Juvenile literature.
2. Cults—United States—History—Juvenile literature. [1. Cults.
2. Religious leaders.] I. Title. II. Series.
BL72.K45 2000
200'.92'2—dc21   99–37857
[B]   CIP

Copyright 2000 by Lucent Books, Inc.
P.O. Box 289011, San Diego, California 92198-9011

Printed in the U.S.A.

CONTENTS

FOREWORD

The literary form most often referred to as "multiple biography" was perfected in the first century A.D. by Plutarch, a perceptive and talented moralist and historian who hailed from the small town of Chaeronea in central Greece. His most famous work, *Parallel Lives*, consists of a long series of biographies of noteworthy ancient Greek and Roman statesmen and military leaders. Frequently, Plutarch compares a famous Greek to a famous Roman, pointing out similarities in personality and achievements. These expertly constructed and very readable tracts provided later historians and others, including playwrights like Shakespeare, with priceless information about prominent ancient personages and also inspired new generations of writers to tackle the multiple biography genre.

The Lucent History Makers series proudly carries on the venerable tradition handed down from Plutarch. Each volume in the series consists of a set of six to eight biographies of important and influential historical figures who were linked together by a common factor. In *Rulers of Ancient Rome*, for example, all the figures were generals, consuls, or emperors of either the Roman Republic or Empire; while the subjects of *Fighters Against American Slavery*, though they lived in different places and times, all shared the same goal, namely the eradication of human servitude. Mindful that politicians and military leaders are not (and never have been) the only people who shape the course of history, the editors of the series have also included representatives from a wide range of endeavors, including scientists, artists, writers, philosophers, religious leaders, and sports figures.

Each book is intended to give a range of figures—some well known, others less known; some who made a great impact on history, others who made only a small impact. For instance, by making Columbus's initial voyage possible, Spain's Queen Isabella I, featured in *Women Leaders of Nations*, helped to open up the New World to exploration and exploitation by the European powers. Unarguably, therefore, she made a major contribution to a series of events that had momentous consequences for the entire world. By contrast, Catherine II, the eighteenth-century Russian queen, and Golda Meir, the modern Israeli prime minister, did not play roles of global impact; however, their policies and actions significantly influenced the historical development of both their own countries and their regional neighbors. Regardless of their relative importance in the greater historical scheme, all of the figures chronicled in the History Makers series made contributions to posterity; and their public achievements, as well as what is known about their private lives, are presented and evaluated in light of the most recent scholarship.

In addition, each volume in the series is documented and substantiated by a wide array of primary and secondary source quotations. The primary source quotes enliven the text by presenting eyewitness views of the times and culture in which each history maker lived; while the secondary source quotes, taken from the works of respected modern scholars, offer expert elaboration and/ or critical commentary. Each quote is footnoted, demonstrating to the reader exactly where biographers find their information. The footnotes also provide the reader with the means of conducting additional research. Finally, to further guide and illuminate readers, each volume in the series features photographs, two bibliographies, and a comprehensive index.

The History Makers series provides both students engaged in research and more casual readers with informative, enlightening, and entertaining overviews of individuals from a variety of circumstances, professions, and backgrounds. No doubt all of them, whether loved or hated, benevolent or cruel, constructive or destructive, will remain endlessly fascinating to each new generation seeking to identify the forces that shaped their world.

Six Charismatic Leaders

Headlines and history books are filled with tales of religious groups whose beliefs and practices stand out as different—and sometimes dangerous—to the rest of society. Some people call these groups "cults"; others prefer more neutral terms like "new religious movements" or "sects." Whichever term one chooses to use, it is essential to remember that no two of these groups are exactly alike. Nor are their leaders.

The six leaders profiled in this book are male and female, rich and poor, young and old, American- and foreign-born. They led groups that were large and small, historic and modern day. Some saw their groups end in horrible tragedy. Others watched as their groups simply ran out of steam. And a few began groups that continued on after the founder's death.

A cult leader's charisma can attract thousands of followers. Here, devotees of Sun Myung Moon fill an arena to hear the religious leader speak.

What, if anything, did these leaders have in common? There are some significant similarities in their sagas. All six made headlines in their day and have earned a place in history—for better or for worse. All six had unusual teachings for which they were fiercely attacked. But perhaps most importantly, all six had *charisma*, a rare human quality that enabled these leaders to attract scores of faithful followers—and to move those followers to do things that many others would consider outrageous. Sun Myung Moon, for example, convinced his believers to spend countless hours begging for change in airports and bus terminals. L. Ron Hubbard persuaded thousands of Scientologists that the one true road to health and happiness was an expensive form of counseling available only through Hubbard's church.

In some cases, a leader's charisma prompted followers to turn over not just their money and time, but their free will in important life decisions. For example, Moon chose spouses for his most loyal followers. David Koresh, head of the Branch Davidians, reportedly controlled virtually every moment of his followers' lives, which ultimately ended in a deadly clash with authorities. And Jim Jones, founder of the infamous Peoples Temple, led hundreds of his followers in a shocking murder-suicide.

This charisma, an unusual ability to capture the trust of fellow human beings, is what binds together the six leaders profiled in this volume. Each chose to use his or her charisma in a distinctive manner, and it is the different uses of the same gift that makes each of the stories unique.

CHAPTER 1

"Cults" and Their Leaders

Although cults have made many headlines in recent years, they are not a new phenomenon. For thousands of years, humans have created groups devoted to particular people or ideas—groups that sometimes have seemed strange or unusual to the rest of the society. For example, some describe the ancient Greek thinker Pythagoras as a cult leader. Pythagoras organized a small group of students and taught them that the study of mathematics could provide answers about the universe. He imposed on his students some very rigid rules. For example, students were expected to live in isolation from the rest of society and to follow a strict vegetarian diet. Pythagoras's students believed in their teacher so deeply, they did whatever he asked.

Many other cults have appeared and disappeared throughout history. Scholars say that especially large numbers of cults pop up at times of social and political unrest—such as periods of war, famine, or economic depression. Why? At times like these, people frequently grow frustrated with life, and they search for answers and guidance. If established religions do not provide that guidance, people often form new religions based on new interpretations of familiar ideas. Because these new religious groups, or cults, frequently go against socially accepted beliefs and practices, they attract criticism and controversy.

What Is a Cult?

Part of the controversy surrounding cults springs from the word itself. *Cult* is hard to define, in part because most people think of the word as an insult. "There is a built-in negative to the word *cult*," remarks Rebecca Moore, a professor of religious studies at the University of North Dakota, who has spent years studying new religious movements. "We only describe people we disapprove of as cultists. And when we call a group a cult, we set the stage for how we will think about them and treat them."[1] Moore argues that the negative images surrounding the word *cult* have stripped the term of any real meaning. Instead, it has simply become an insulting label.

Originally, cult had a neutral (neither positive nor negative) meaning. It comes from the Latin word *cultus*, which in ancient Rome meant a group showing intense devotion to a person, place, thing, or idea. Under this broad definition, a cult could be a group of people who support a particular political idea or a group of fans dedicated to a particular musician.

Today, cult has at least three competing definitions. One definition arose in the early twentieth century among conservative Christian leaders, who used the word to describe any religion that differed from traditional Christian teachings. Their definition would include all the world's other prominent religions, including Judaism and Islam. It would also include groups that broke away from traditional Christian churches because of a disagreement over teachings. Some conservative Christian groups continue to apply this definition today to such denominations as Latter-day Saints (Mormons) and Jehovah's Witnesses.

A second definition of cult comes from what is known as the anticult movement. Most members of the anticult movement are secular, or nonreligious, people who define cults by how members live and behave rather than what they believe. The anticult movement sprang up in the 1960s and 1970s, when many young people felt lost in society and turned to new religions for answers. Some joined religious movements that required unusual practices such as communal living. Then, many parents and families, alarmed by the possibility that their relatives were being tricked, or brainwashed, started the anticult movement to make others aware of what they considered dangerous cult groups. They also came up with their own definition. According to anticultists, all cults share some common characteristics. They demand that members swear allegiance to an all-powerful leader,

Pythagoras, the renowned Greek philosopher and mathematician, is considered by some to have been an early cult leader.

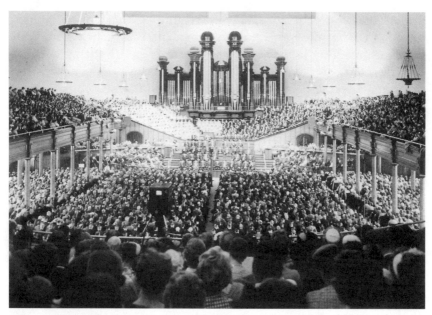

Latter-day Saints worship in the Mormon Tabernacle in Salt Lake City. Even today, some conservative Christians consider Mormonism to be a cult.

they discourage independent thought, and they create rigid rules dictating how members live. According to the anticultists, cults also use deceptive practices to lure members into the various groups and to isolate members from the outside world, so that they will become completely dependent on the group. This rigid lifestyle and distrust of outsiders combine to make all cults potentially violent, anticultists say.

At first glance, the anticultists' definition seems concrete and easy to use. To identify a cult, one simply has to go down the checklist, looking for the telltale traits. But many experts say that the definition has some weaknesses. Religious scholar J. Gordon Melton points out that this definition was based not on objective research but on parents' perceptions of their children's behavior. Morton also notes that anticultists have used their definition to make all cult groups sound destructive—and to attract support for their fight against all cults. He writes that because of the anticult movement, " 'cults' have come to be seen as groups that share a variety of generally destructive characteristics." [2] The problem is that these characteristics can be hard to measure. For example, an anticultist may see the members of a group as overly dependent, but the members themselves may describe a wonderful feeling of community. Because of this difficulty in agreeing on subjective qualities, the anticultists' definition is not the one used by most scholars. However, it *is* the definition that is used most frequently by the general public and the media.

The third definition is the one used by most historians and social scientists. These scholars define a cult as a religious group that is foreign to the one or more existing religious communities. That is, a cult is a group whose beliefs and practices are very different from those of others in the community as a whole. According to social scientists, cults can form in a variety of ways. Some break away from established religions because they have a new and different perspective on old teachings. Other cults form around a belief that has no roots in an existing religion. Still other cults are religions from a different time or place that gradually take root in a community. For example, when Buddhism first made its way into the United States, it was considered a cult by many Americans—even though it had been practiced in the East for thousands of years.

Social scientists emphasize that when they use the term *cult*, it is meant to be neutral and nonjudgmental. To them, the word simply refers to the way a religious group relates to its surrounding community. They acknowledge that some cults may ultimately prove destructive or dangerous, but many others will not.

When Buddhism was first introduced to the United States, many Americans viewed the ancient religion as a cult based on Buddha (pictured).

From Cult to Religion

Another factor that makes it difficult to define a cult is that according to some experts, many large religious groups began as cults or had the characteristics of a cult at some point in their history. For example, the first Christians were deeply faithful followers of Jesus of Nazareth who believed that their teacher had risen from the dead. Moses, a great leader in Jewish history, won the faith of the Hebrew people when he reported that God had appeared to him. And Islamic people had faith in their leader, Mohammed, when he said that his teachings came directly from Allah, or God.

In all these instances, the early believers had tremendous faith in the teachings of their leader, but other people in their communities found the groups' beliefs strange and unacceptable. Now, however, these one-time cults are mainstream religions.

Cult Leaders

Whichever definition of a cult one chooses to use, a strong leader is a vital part of the picture. A dynamic leader is important in any religious group. In a religious group whose beliefs or customs differ radically from the outside community, such a leader is possibly the most essential ingredient. Because the group's practices may seem bizarre and destructive to the outside world, the group frequently faces ridicule and criticism. A powerful leader helps hold his or her group together in the face of such opposition. For example, Mother Ann Lee and her Shaker followers were arrested time after time because of their beliefs, but Lee reassured her followers that the opposition they faced would only make them stronger.

What is it about a cult leader that makes followers willing to hand over their trust, time, and free will? Almost all these leaders share the quality called *charisma*. A charismatic person is usually

The leader of a South Pacific cult erects a cross atop an active volcano. To outsiders, such practices may seem bizarre and inappropriate.

a convincing and powerful speaker, one who draws others to him or her like a magnet. However, there is also a religious component to this trait. *Charisma* comes from the Greek word for "divine gift." Even today, when religious scholars say that a cult leader is charismatic, they mean that the leader claims to have some sort of special communication or link with a divine being.

For many cult leaders, this link comes in the form of visions. The Reverend Sun Myung Moon, leader of the Unification Church, claims to have had countless visions of God, Jesus, and Buddha. He is not alone; the other leaders profiled in this book all reported having visions of some kind, providing them with answers to life's mysteries or telling them what actions to take. Charismatic cult leaders often call themselves prophets or divine messengers. Some even call themselves God. Charisma, however, is in the eye of the believer. An average person may look at a cult leader and see nothing special; a believer may look at the same person and see a wise prophet. An outsider may dismiss a cult leader as crazy; a cult insider may call that same individual God. As long as a cult leader has enough followers who believe his or her claims, the cult can flourish.

In addition to posessing an undeniably high level of charisma, cult leaders often claim to have extraordinary gifts or powers. For example, Mother Ann Lee claimed to be able to see through to a person's soul and detect any sins the person had failed to confess. David Koresh taught that he alone had the gift of interpreting the Bible correctly.

Psychological Characteristics

Charisma and claims of extraordinary powers help to separate a cult leader from an ordinary minister of faith. In addition, cult leaders tend to share an interesting set of psychological characteristics. According to English psychiatrist and author Anthony Storr, charismatic spiritual leaders (whom he calls gurus) seldom have close friends; in fact, having close friendships would detract from the leader's air of mystery and authority by making him or her seem more normal and human. As Storr writes, "[The leaders] tend to be more interested in what goes on inside their own minds than in personal relationships, perhaps because they do not believe that anyone else really cares for them."[3] Cult leaders also tend to be intolerant of criticism; they see people as supporters or enemies, with little or no middle ground. Additionally, Storr suggests that charismatic cult leaders have an intense conviction in their beliefs—at least at the beginning. That is, although cult leaders

Although outsiders may easily dismiss the claims of a cult leader, devoted followers like this woman may behold the leader as a prophet who can unlock life's mysteries or as a messiah who can commune with supreme beings.

do not necessarily believe *everything* they preach, they do believe that they have some special insight. Rather than discuss his or her ideas, a leader simply imposes those ideas on others.

Traits like charisma and intensity of conviction combine to give a cult leader a great deal of power. Such power can be dangerous— but it need not be.

Cult Leaders and Religious Freedom

When a cult leader makes the news for preaching strange ideas or encouraging unusual practices, some may wonder why the group is not banned or stopped. The answer, at least in the United States, is freedom of religion. The First Amendment to the U.S. Constitution begins by stating, "Congress shall make no law respecting an establishment of religion, or prohibiting the free exercise thereof." That means that unless a group that identifies itself as religious is breaking the law, government cannot interfere.

With this strong constitutional protection, new religious movements of many different kinds have appeared in the United States. Their leaders have preached all kinds of messages: that the end of the world is coming, that religion can erase the world's problems, even that humans would be saved by a flying saucer from outer space. They have made their case passionately, convincingly, and in some instances quite memorably.

CHAPTER 2

Mother Ann Lee:
The Shakers

"I love Mother,
I love her power,
I know it 'twill
Help me in every trying hour . . ."[4]

These words, taken from a two-hundred-year-old Shaker hymn, show the deep faith the people known as Shakers had in their first leader, Mother Ann Lee. Although Lee and her followers were initially persecuted for their unusual beliefs, the leader had established almost a dozen Shaker settlements throughout the northeastern United States by the end of the eighteenth century.

Today, many historians remember Mother Ann Lee as one of the most effective female preachers of all time. A powerful speaker and dynamic leader, Mother Ann inspired countless followers to abandon traditional family life and join her settlements. But more than two centuries ago, Mother Ann's neighbors and enemies had a very different view. They saw Lee as a strange person whose beliefs did not match those of the rest of society. Not only did Mother Ann claim to communicate with God, she was also a woman—and in the eighteenth century people were unaccustomed to seeing women in positions of great power. Because of this, Mother Ann was persecuted, arrested, and ordered out of many communities.

Early Years

Ann Lee was born in Manchester, England, on February 29, 1736. Ann's father, John, was a blacksmith who worked day and night to support his family. Little is known about Ann's mother; since women were considered unimportant to a family line, her name was not even recorded on Ann's birth records. The Lees lived on Toad Lane, a dirty, rat-infested street in a poor neighborhood.

Ann was the second of eight children. Like most other working-class children in Manchester, she did not attend school and never

As a child, Ann Lee endured long days and much hardship in a Manchester clothing mill.

learned to read or write. Instead, she went to work in the local clothing mills to help earn money for her family. From the time she turned eight years old, she worked twelve hours a day cutting strips of velvet and preparing cotton for the looms.

When Ann was twenty-two years old, she went to work as a cook in a hospital. Around the same time, she met a couple named James and Jane Wardley and became interested in religion. The couple had started their own small church called the Wardley Society. The Wardleys had a lot in common with the Quakers, a religious group that believed in private reflection and simple living.

But they also were influenced by a group called the French Prophets, who were known for speaking in mysterious languages and falling into trances. Like the French Prophets, the Wardleys believed that Jesus would soon return to earth. They believed that this time, Jesus would appear as a woman.

Ann found the Wardley Society very different from the Church of England, which she considered too "stuffy," or formal. She wanted a religion that had more meaning for poor, common people, and the Wardley Society fit the bill. The Wardley Society meetings were exciting and intense with each one including a period of silent reflection, public confessions of sins, and an enthusiastic sermon. Then the meeting would end with chanting, singing, and dancing. Sometimes the society members were so moved by their faith that they began to shake wildly. Before long, this behavior earned the group a nickname, the "Shaking Quakers."

When Ann was twenty-six years old, her father felt it was time she had a home and family of her own and forced her to marry a blacksmith named Abraham Standerin. The next few years were very painful for Ann. She and Abraham had four children, all of whom died in early childhood. Although infant mortality was very high in those days because of disease and poor medical care, Ann blamed herself for her children's deaths. She was overcome with grief and guilt, and she began to believe that God was punishing her for having married Abraham.

Ann's grief made her grow very thin and weak. But as time passed, she found comfort and strength in the Wardley Society. Ann soon turned all of her attention to religion and assumed a more active role in the group. She prayed constantly and began to lead some of the meetings. As one biographer notes, this was an important turning point in Ann's life:

> Following the death of her last child in October 1766, [Ann] assumed a more zealous role in the Wardley order. During her ordeal, the Wardleys had been a source of personal comfort, and their meetings a means of emotional release. But once her health was restored, participation was infused with a sense of mission.[5]

A Leader in the Making

As Ann became more active in the Shaking Quakers, she began to attract the attention of local authorities. She and other Shaking Quakers were arrested several times for "disturbing the peace" with their meetings. Each time, Ann was thrown into a cold, stone cell in the Manchester prison. Each time, she came out with renewed faith. According to one researcher,

> Abuse did not dishearten Ann; far from it. The more she was mistreated, the more intense her soul-searching and her religious conviction grew. She intended to preach the Gospel and to help others find God . . . and nothing was going to stop her.[6]

During one prison stay in 1770, as she prayed feverishly in her cell, Ann claimed to have had a vision in which she saw God and learned the reason for human suffering. According to Ann, God revealed that the root of all sin was the sexual relationship between Adam and Eve, the first man and woman. Ann now believed that celibacy, or abstaining from sex, even within marriage, was the key to salvation.

When Ann was released from prison, she shared the story of her vision with the Wardleys. They were so convinced that what Ann said was true that they made her the new leader of the group. Under Ann's leadership, the group became known as the United Society of Believers in Christ's Second Coming. However, most people simply called the followers the "Shakers."

In the early 1770s, Ann and other Shakers began speaking out against the Church of England for encouraging marriage. To many

Members of the Wardley Society, known as the Shaking Quakers, dance and sing during one of their emotion-filled meetings.

Ann's radical beliefs led to her confinement to a mental asylum. While there, she claimed to have been visited by Jesus Christ.

outsiders, their stand against marriage was absurd. On July 14, 1772, constables stormed a meeting that Ann was leading in her father's house. They arrested Ann, her father, and several others for creating a public nuisance. The prisoners were released after several weeks, but Ann immediately resumed her controversial preaching and was arrested again within the year. According to an old Shaker story, Ann was put in a tiny cell with no food or water. Fourteen days later, when authorities opened the cell, they were surprised to find that she had survived. According to the story, a young follower named James Whittaker had rescued Ann by delivering a mixture of milk and wine through a keyhole. Because of incidents like this one, the Shakers began to believe their leader was invincible.

A few months later, Ann Lee was arrested again and thrown into an asylum, or home for the mentally ill. According to Ann, Jesus Christ appeared to her in the asylum and told her that *she* was the second coming of Christ, the female savior the Wardleys had predicted would appear. When Ann was released, she told the rest of the Shakers about her vision. They believed her, and began to call her Mother Ann.

Mother Ann taught the Shakers that they must confess all sins, remain celibate, and work hard if they wanted to be saved from sin. Although the Shakers did not worship Mother Ann as God, they believed in her teachings and considered Ann and Jesus together to be the most important figures in their church.

The New World

In 1773, after telling her followers that she had received a message from God directing the Shakers to move to America, Mother Ann began organizing for the journey. Eight Shakers were able to settle their affairs in England and make the trip. Among them were Ann's brother, William, and her husband, Abraham, who had remained with Ann even though their marriage had become strained.

Although most of the Shakers were poor laborers and housewives, a few were well-to-do businessmen. Mother Ann asked one of the wealthier followers, John Hocknell, to make the financial arrangements for the journey. Passage to America for nine people was quite expensive, and the only ship Hocknell could afford was the recently condemned *Mariah*. However, the Shakers were confident that they would be safe aboard the sagging ship, and on May 19, 1774, Mother Ann and her eight followers set sail from Liverpool, England.

The journey to America took three long months, and conditions on board the *Mariah* were almost unbearable. The passenger areas of the ship had no fresh air and little clean water for drinking and bathing. With no way to keep food cold, the Shakers dined on spoiled meat and vegetables. In addition, unpredictable winds and weather made the trip a rough one. Despite these conditions, Mother Ann and her group worshiped, sang, and danced on board the ship. The crew and captain grew irritated.

According to a story handed down among the Shakers, tensions on board the boat mounted until one stormy night, when the *Mariah* sprang a leak and began to take on water at an alarming rate. The crew panicked, but Mother Ann reassured them that everyone would be safe. "Not a hair of our heads shall perish and we shall arrive safely in America," Ann promised. "For I was just now sitting by the mast, and I saw a bright angel of God, through whom I received the promise."[7] According to the story, the ship's crew trusted Mother Ann, and, with her help, worked to pump the water from the decks.

Mother Ann and her followers arrived in New York on August 6, 1774. The Shakers knew not a single person in America and had no place to live, but Mother Ann was not worried. She and the others simply walked down a New York street and knocked on the door of a house. When the lady of the house, Mrs. Cunningham, answered, Mother Ann asked for permission to stay, saying an angel had directed her to the house. The Cunninghams invited Ann and her husband into their home and gave them jobs in the household. The other Shakers found lodging with families nearby.

Mother Ann knew the accommodations were only temporary, and she asked three Shaker men to begin looking for a more permanent settlement. The men eventually found a large plot of land in a village called Niskeyuna, about eight miles northwest of Albany, New York. The Shakers leased the property and began clearing the land. Then they set to work building a log cabin with two floors, one for the Shaker men, and the other for the Shaker women.

While the Niskeyuna settlement was being built, Mother Ann remained in the city. She washed and ironed clothes for the Cunninghams and cared for Abraham, who had fallen ill. In 1775 the couple divorced and Ann fell into poverty. By spring of 1776, however, the settlement was ready and Ann and the other Shakers who had remained in New York City journeyed up the Hudson River to their new home.

Living in Niskeyuna was not easy. The Shakers had to drain swampy areas on the property and plant crops. In the beginning, food was scarce and everyone was sick. But Mother Ann and the Shakers worked hard and gradually made a home for themselves. They hoped their small community would soon expand, so they kept enough food and provisions for a large group.

When several years passed and the Shaker community still had not grown, Mother Ann was disappointed. The Shakers worshiped together several times a day and prayed for their tiny church to grow. Soon, their prayers were answered.

A Shaker Awakening

The Shakers had arrived in the colonies in the middle of a wave of religious expression known as the Great Awakening. As the name suggests, the Great Awakening was a time of renewed interest in religion. At the time, many people believed that "judgment day," or the end of the world, would come soon, and they wanted to be ready. During the Great Awakening, people held frequent religious gatherings known as revivals. They gathered at the revivals to talk about the best way to achieve salvation.

In March 1780 a large revival meeting was held in New Lebanon, New York, not far from the Niskeyuna settlement. Afterward, two men who had been to the revival headed home in the direction of Niskeyuna. On their way, they happened upon the Shaker settlement, and Mother Ann Lee invited them to spend the night. The next day, the men watched the Shakers worship and talked to Mother Ann about her teachings. The men were impressed with Mother Ann's message that celibacy and the public confession of sins would save their souls.

The two men helped spread the word about Mother Ann Lee and her Shaker community, and by May people were coming in droves to hear Mother Ann preach. They filled the cabin from top to bottom and spilled over to the outside. Mother Ann held as many as three meetings a day to give each newcomer a chance to participate in Shaker worship. Many of the newcomers decided to stay at Niskeyuna permanently.

As the settlement grew, Mother Ann made the rules of her community very clear. Shakers were to take no pride in their appearance and wear only the plainest of clothes. Instead of owning fancy homes full of expensive furniture, they had to live communally in the simple Shaker settlement. They were to make and grow everything they needed and shun life on the outside, which Ann called "the World." Shakers could not waste food or turn away the poor. And, above all, they had to commit themselves to celibacy, confession, and hard work.

During the Great Awakening, religious revival meetings attracted numerous followers who hoped to attain salvation before the end of the world.

Mother Ann established several rules of conduct. Among them, Shakers were not to take pride in their appearance and were to dress in very plain, simple clothing (pictured).

Why were so many people willing to make these sacrifices? "Mother Ann was inspirational," says Todd Burdick, director of education at the Hancock Shaker Village, a Shaker museum in Massachusetts. "She was able to move people both emotionally and spiritually."[8] And, at the Shaker prayer meetings, Mother Ann was even able to move her followers physically. Trances, shaking, dancing, and singing were all common occurrences at Shaker meetings. As one visitor to Niskeyuna wrote in 1780:

> When they meet together for their worship, they fall a groaning and trembling, and every one acts alone for himself; one will fall prostrate on the floor, another on his knees and his head in his hands.[9]

In addition, Mother Ann claimed to have several gifts from God. She said she was able to see the unconfessed sins on a person's soul and to heal the sick. Many Shaker converts believed that Mother Ann had cured their fevers, broken bones, and other ailments.

Wartime Trouble

Eventually, Mother Ann Lee encountered conflict in America, just as she had in England. Her meetings and religious teachings were unusual enough to attract attention throughout New England. Her claim that she was the female Christ and her belief in celibacy were especially controversial. However, what attracted the most criticism in revolutionary America was Mother Ann's teaching that all violence and fighting were wrong. Mother Ann reportedly urged followers to "Arm yourselves only with meekness and patience." [10] This belief, called pacifism, made Mother Ann unpopular among patriotic colonists, and rumors began to spread that the Shaker leader was hiding British spies at Niskeyuna.

In the summer of 1780, Mother Ann and several other Shakers were arrested by the New York militia and charged with "disloyalty to the American cause." Mother Ann insisted that her group played no role in the war against England. She was asked to take an oath pledging her support to America, but she refused. After she had spent several months in prison, some Shaker supporters appealed to the governor of New York for her release. Governor George Clinton said he would grant the release if Mother Ann would promise not to jeopardize the safety of the colonies. Mother Ann promised and was set free. Although rumors continued that she was a British supporter, she was able to return to Niskeyuna and concentrate on her preaching.

Growth of the Shakers

Because the Shakers did not have any children, spreading their beliefs to newcomers was the only way to make the community grow. Back at Niskeyuna, Mother Ann continued to hold public meetings in order to win new converts. Then, in 1781, she decided to take her teachings on the road. In May of that year, she and five followers set out for the Northeast.

Mother Ann convinced many people to join the Shaker movement in her travels, but she also stirred up suspicion and distrust. When Mother Ann arrived in a town to preach, angry mobs often appeared. People worried that Mother Ann would "steal" members of communities and break up families. And Mother Ann had still not lost her reputation as a British supporter.

One of Ann's most successful stops was Harvard, Massachusetts. She arrived in Harvard in June 1781, and before long had established a community of more than one hundred Shakers. But she did less well in neighboring towns. When Ann arrived in the town of Petersham, she discovered that her enemies were waiting for her. A rumor had spread in Petersham that Mother Ann was not a woman at all, but a man wearing a disguise. One night, while Mother Ann was conducting a Shaker meeting, some members of the Petersham militia stormed the house and dragged her away. Then they interrogated her and forced her to take off her clothes. Only when they were convinced that Mother Ann was indeed a woman did they release her. However, they demanded that the Shakers leave town immediately.

Mother Ann decided to cut her travels short and lead the Shakers back to Niskeyuna. However, when they reached the town of New Lebanon, New York, Mother Ann was arrested for her teachings and hauled into court. After hearing the charismatic woman speak, the judge agreed to release her on bond, but Ann did not make it very far. As she climbed into her carriage to go, a crowd attacked her and beat her severely.

Mother Ann's Last Year

The long travels and the beating in New Lebanon had taken their toll, and when Ann returned to Niskeyuna in September 1783, she was frail and ill. As one biographer notes, "They had been gone two years and four months, traveled hundreds of miles, and suffered indescribable hardship and persecution."[11] But Mother Ann had accomplished her mission: She had introduced Shakerism into many new communities in New England.

In July 1784 Ann's beloved brother William died, and Ann grew even more sad and weary. She seemed to have a premonition of her own death, and she began instructing her followers on how to run the Shaker settlements. On September 8, 1784, she passed

Shakers sing during a meeting in New York. During one such meeting in Petersham, Massachusetts, Mother Ann was carried off by angry members of the town militia.

After Mother Ann's death, the Shakers continued to follow her teachings and expanded their communities, enlarging meeting halls to accommodate their growing numbers.

away at the age of forty-eight. The *Albany Gazette* published the news of Mother Ann's death, and Shakers from all over New England arrived for their leader's funeral services. At the funeral, faithful follower James Whittaker assured the Shakers that Ann's entry into the spirit world was necessary for her continued work.

Under Whittaker's leadership, the Shakers survived this rocky period and even expanded. By the 1800s, there were eighteen Shaker communities spread all over the United States. Eventually, they became known less for their controversial views and more for their simple living and hard work. Today, as people visit quaint Shaker museums and pay high prices for Shaker-made antiques, it is easy to forget the swirl of controversy that once surrounded the group and its charismatic leader, Mother Ann Lee.

CHAPTER 3

Father Divine: The Universal Peace Mission Movement

In the decades between World Wars I and II, an African-American preacher who was called Father Divine took America by storm. Father Divine led his followers to believe that he was God. And, unlike many ministers, he did not preach that suffering on earth would be rewarded in heaven. Instead, Father Divine taught impoverished blacks that if they worked hard, sought God, and took charge of their lives, they could overcome racism and achieve success here on earth. That, Father Divine said, was the *real* heaven.

To help his followers toward that goal, Father Divine offered job opportunities and meals to all who knocked on his door.

Although Father Divine attracted his share of controversy, his message and meals caught on quickly among both blacks and whites. He became a household name in major cities like New York, Los Angeles, and Philadelphia. Perhaps one anecdote introduces Father Divine's story best of all. According to several researchers, a letter once arrived in the post office in Harlem, New York City. It was addressed simply to God, Harlem, U.S.A. Without a second thought, the postmaster arranged to have the mysterious letter delivered to Father Divine.

Father Divine, the preacher who brought hope to destitute Americans between the 1910s and the 1960s.

Life on Middle Lane

Because Father Divine never shared the details of his early life, historians have had to piece together the story of the preacher's childhood from public documents. However, it is known that Father Divine's real name was George Baker and that he was the son of Nancy and George Baker Sr. Both Nancy and George Sr. had been slaves until 1864. According to some historians, George Jr. was born in Savannah, Georgia, in 1880. According to others, he was born in Rockville, Maryland, in 1879. Whichever version is correct, Rockville is where George spent most of his childhood.

In the late 1800s, black people in Maryland enjoyed some rights they did not have in other southern states. For example, black men in Maryland were allowed to vote and own land. Even so, racism and segregation were rampant. In the small town of Rockville, the black and white populations were completely separated. Whites lived in the center of town, while the Bakers and other black residents lived in a ghetto called Middle Lane.

The Bakers and another family shared a small log cabin on Middle Lane. It was hard to make ends meet. Nancy Baker was obese and unable to find work, and George Sr. supported his family by doing yard work for white families. Young George attended a one-room public school that Rockville had set aside for black students. There, students used old textbooks, desks, and other supplies thrown away by the town's white schools. Despite these difficult conditions, George learned to read and write. He at-

Bordered by train tracks, this poverty-stricken slum housed many of Baltimore's poorer blacks during the late nineteenth and early twentieth centuries.

tended school until his teenage years, when he began working odd jobs for twenty-five cents a day to help support his family.

Although the Baker family lacked money, they enjoyed a rich community life. Rockville's close-knit African-American community held frequent picnics, dances, and other gatherings. The community also shared religious services; many of Rockville's black residents were Methodists, and they worshiped together on Sundays. George participated in his community, especially its religious life. Biographer Jill Watts notes:

> He spent his Sundays in church school and worship services, his weeknights at prayer meetings and Bible study. . . . Inevitably, the intense spirituality and religious dedication of the African-American community left a deep impression on George.[12]

Early Ministry

In 1899 Baker moved to Baltimore, Maryland's largest city. Here he encountered a large number of African Americans living in two different worlds. Some of Baltimore's African Americans—those who were doctors and ministers—lived in middle-class comfort. Others lived in extremely poor conditions in downtown alleys or near the dirty Baltimore docks.

Baker did not have the money to join the middle class, nor did he have any desire to live in poverty. His prospects looked grim. Then he found lodging in the home of an elderly white man named William Ortwine. Baker began doing gardening work in the neighborhood for fifty cents a day and roomed with Ortwine's household staff.

Once settled in Baltimore, Baker again turned to religion. In addition to several large African-American churches, Baltimore boasted a number of small churches that were not connected to any of the major denominations. Baker joined one of these "storefront churches" and eventually took turns preaching and teaching Sunday school.

While praying and preaching in the storefront church, Baker began to think a lot about the conditions in which most African Americans were living. He was tired of being told that the problems blacks experienced because of racism and poverty would be erased in heaven. George Baker thought the idea of heaven was simply too far away; in fact, he was not sure such a place existed at all. He wanted to find a way to improve African Americans' lives here and now. This message began to appear in Baker's sermons.

Around the same time, Baker also discovered a philosophy called "New Thought." New Thought was the idea that God's spirit was inside every human being and that by tuning in to God's presence, a person could achieve health and success. Baker was especially intrigued with the New Thought idea that God was in *all* people: poor or rich, white or black. This message, too, became part of his sermons.

Traveling Preacher

Baker had grown to enjoy preaching, and in 1902 he decided to strike out on his own. He first headed south, stopping in many towns and cities to share his blossoming ideas. In 1906 Baker visited Los Angeles, where New Thought was very popular. During his trip, Baker experienced what he described as a spiritual rebirth. He said he felt called to leave his old life and identity behind, and begin a new life spreading his message far and wide.

When Baker returned to Baltimore later that year, it did not take long for him to create his new identity. While worshiping at a storefront church called the Eden Street Church, he met a man named Samuel Morris. Morris horrified others in the church by claiming to be God. But Baker was fascinated with Morris's claim. If people could have God's spirit inside them, he thought, why couldn't a person be God? So Baker teamed up with Morris and began calling himself "The Messenger, God in the Sonship Degree." Together, the two men preached around their Baltimore neighborhood.

It was not long before bickering broke out between the preachers. They could not agree on how to interpret certain passages in the Bible or, just as importantly, how to run their ministry. In 1912 the Messenger announced that he—not Morris—was the true embodiment of God. It was the final straw in their relationship, and the men parted ways.

The Messenger was committed to spreading his ideas of self-help and positive thinking and once again he traveled south. He found that many people—especially African Americans—were very eager to listen. Although American blacks had been freed from slavery for almost fifty years, opportunities and rights in the South were very limited. The Messenger's teaching about heaven on earth gave his believers a feeling of hope. Many began to believe they had the potential to change their own lives.

As he traveled, the Messenger refused to accept donations of money, but he gladly accepted food and lodging. Once invited into a believer's home, he would conduct worship services there. Each service included preaching, singing, and a giant meal. The Messenger called these meals Holy Communion banquets. Over time, they would become one of the most important aspects of his church.

The Messenger attracted his share of critics along with believers. In several places, he clashed with local ministers, who said he was not trained as a preacher. In 1913 he was arrested for getting into an argument with local ministers in Savannah, Georgia, and served two months in prison. When he was released in the beginning of 1914, the Messenger moved on to another Georgia city, Valdosta. There, he held services in people's homes and attracted a sizable following. Most of the followers were black women, who at that time held very low status in southern society. The women were astounded by the Messenger's teaching that they should take control of their lives. The men of the community were equally astounded—and complained loudly about the new preacher in town. In February 1914, just weeks after arriving in Valdosta, the Messenger was arrested on charges of "lunacy." At his trial, several black men testified that the Messenger was crazy. They said that the Messenger had claimed to be God and had stirred up the

As a traveling preacher, the Messenger (center) conducted worship services, or Holy Communion banquets, in the homes of his followers, many of whom were women.

women of the community. However, a talented lawyer helped with the case, and the court agreed to drop the charges if the Messenger would leave town.

The Messenger had several more clashes with the law as he continued to preach around the country. From 1914 to 1917 he visited many southern and northern cities but rarely stayed in one place for more than a month. He eventually attracted a loyal band of six to twelve people who followed him from town to town.

New York Settlements

In 1917 the Messenger decided to establish his ministry in New York City, a place he had visited during his travels. He rented an apartment for himself and his followers in Brooklyn, one of the city's five boroughs. There, the Messenger opened his door to anyone in need. He helped his followers find jobs and made sure they had enough to eat. He continued to host the elaborate Holy Communion dinners he had begun in the South. In return, he expected his followers to obey certain rules. There were to be no relationships between men and women. Smoking, alcohol, drugs, and foul language were all banned. And every able-bodied person in the settlement had to work and contribute some of his or her wages to the community.

Among those living in the Brooklyn community was a woman named Penniniah, who suffered from a crippling disease called rheumatism. She was one of the Messenger's most dedicated followers, and he chose her as his wife. They claimed that their relationship was spiritual, not physical, and no one in the community doubted it. Like the Messenger himself, Penniniah was much loved by the small group of followers.

At the time of his marriage, the Messenger changed his name to the Reverend Major Jealous Divine. According to his biographers, he combined the religious title "Reverend" and the military title "Major" because both words conveyed authority. He took the word "Jealous" from a passage in the Bible: "Thou shalt worship no other god. For the Lord . . . is a jealous God." And he used the word "Divine" to remind his followers that he was God. Ignoring the long title, most followers simply called their leader Father Divine—a nickname that would stick with him the rest of his life.

In October 1919 Father Divine decided that his followers needed to escape from the city's problems. For a little over $3,000, Divine and his wife purchased a home in Sayville, Long Island, a suburb of New York City. They were the town's first African-American homeowners. Although Sayville was isolated, historians

After settling in New York, Father Divine continued to host Holy Communion banquets that attracted hordes of followers of all races and ages.

believe Divine considered it the perfect place for his ministry to grow. One researcher notes:

> By distancing his disciples from other religious orders, familiar surroundings, and previous companions, Father Divine eliminated many of the temptations luring away converts and increased his followers' allegiance to and dependence on him.[13]

On the surface, Divine's move to Long Island seems to make little sense. Some biographers say that Divine made the move for what he believed was his followers' own good. That is, Divine may have believed that only he could help his followers change their lives. On the other hand, Divine's motive may have been to gather power for himself.

On Long Island, Father Divine continued to help the needy. He called his home "the Refuge Home for the Poor Only" and opened its doors to anyone in need. Some hungry people came only for the lavish Holy Communion banquets. Others stayed for a few weeks while Divine helped them find jobs. Still others were so impressed with Divine's teachings that they decided to move in permanently.

For eight years, Father Divine's group grew slowly. Then, in the late 1920s, the number of followers skyrocketed. In October

1929 the American stock market crashed, sending the country into the economic tailspin called the Great Depression. Millions of Americans were without savings, jobs, and homes. The hard times made Father Divine's free meals very appealing to blacks and whites alike.

Problems Arise

By 1930 there were between thirty and sixty people living in Father Divine's home. For the first time, Father Divine's neighbors began to complain to the authorities. The neighbors claimed that Divine's group was making too much noise. And as Divine began to put additions on his house and buy fancy cars, neighbors wondered where he got the money.

That spring, authorities sent an undercover agent into Divine's home to learn more about him. The agent, a young black woman, spent some time with Divine's group and finally issued a report that was printed in local newspapers. According to the report, Divine was a harmless preacher who did not even take donations from his followers. All of the group's money, the report claimed, came from honest work.

Despite this positive report, the public debate over Father Divine continued. Thanks to the ongoing publicity, an average of six hundred people began attending the preacher's Holy Communion banquets each Sunday. Because Father Divine could seat only fifty or sixty people at a time, the visitors had to take turns. They waited outside in cars and buses.

By mid-November of 1931 the tensions in Sayville finally boiled over. Responding to neighbors' complaints about the heavy traffic and nonstop noise, police arrested Father Divine and seventy of his followers for "creating a public nuisance." More than half of those arrested pleaded guilty to the charge and were released after paying fines. But Divine and thirty-two others pleaded not guilty and were jailed while they waited for a trial.

In the spring of 1932 Father Divine was convicted and stood before Judge Lewis Smith to be sentenced. Judge Smith had made no secret of his contempt for the defendant, and it was no surprise when he sentenced Divine to a year in jail and a $500 fine.

Several days after handing down Father Divine's sentence, however, Judge Smith died of a heart attack. For Divine, the timing of Smith's death could not have been better. Divine's followers began to murmur that their powerful leader had used supernatural powers to cause Smith's death. Father Divine himself even stated from his prison cell, "I hated to do it." [14] After

Smith's death, Father Divine appealed his sentence, claiming that it was too harsh. A higher court agreed.

God of Harlem

Father Divine and his followers left Sayville in 1932 and returned to New York City. They settled in Harlem, a section of the city with a large and flourishing African-American community. For many years, Father Divine would use Harlem as his base. He set up a home like the one he had run in Sayville and called it the "Peace Mission." According to cult expert J. Gordon Melton, the mission was a success. Melton writes, "[Divine] had become a hero to the black community. . . . Members were able, through the Mission's assistance, to have cheap food, shelter, a job, and a reformed life." [15] Because of his work, Father Divine won the nickname "God of Harlem." His group also took on a new name: the Universal Peace Mission Movement.

In the early 1930s the Peace Mission Movement began to spread nationwide. Followers printed pamphlets and organized banquets as far away as California. Soon, more than a hundred Peace Missions had popped up all over the country. Most were

Father Divine's Peace Missions offered food, shelter, and jobs to the needy. As the movement grew, Divine opened low-cost Peace Mission restaurants and markets (pictured).

large homes where followers lived and worshiped together. By 1935, a few Peace Missions had appeared in Europe, Canada, Australia, and the West Indies.

As the Peace Mission Movement grew, Father Divine proved to be a shrewd businessman. First, he set up several New York City restaurants offering hot meals at low prices. Later, Father Divine opened low-cost hotels and markets. To provide food for these businesses, Divine had his followers buy some farmland in upstate New York. The followers called the farm the Promised Land.

Father Divine made sure all of his businesses followed certain rules: (1) always have low prices; (2) never accept tips; (3) do not let customers buy on credit, because they will end up in debt; and (4) do not sell liquor or tobacco. Father Divine's followers ran the businesses on these principles, and the profits poured in. The money helped keep the Peace Mission Movement afloat. To avoid being criticized for profiting from his movement, Father Divine made sure that the businesses were in his followers' names rather than his own.

Business was not Father Divine's only experiment. In the mid-1930s, Divine also tried his hand at politics. Just before the 1936 presidential election, Divine announced his political views and challenged the major presidential candidates to support those positions. Although the candidates believed that Divine could help them win African-American votes, they were scared off by Divine's controversial political stands. Divine had called for an end to the death penalty and a ban on all bombs and other weapons. He also demanded an end to racism and school segregation. Since none of the candidates would support his views, Father Divine urged all of his followers to stay home on Election Day—and many did. After the election, Divine continued to spread his political viewpoint through Peace Mission magazines.

A Broken Peace

For years critics had claimed that Father Divine was a fraud who used his followers for his own financial gain. Until the late 1930s, none of these charges had stuck to Divine and his Peace Mission. Then the preacher faced a series of crises that damaged his reputation forever.

In 1936 a Peace Mission follower named John Huest Hunt fell in love with the seventeen-year-old daughter of another follower. Hunt took the minor to California and was later charged with kidnapping. The girl's family sold the story to the newspapers, and Father Divine could not shake the negative publicity.

The father of the kidnapped seventeen-year-old reads about his daughter's case in the New York Journal. *The scandal rocked Father Divine's Peace Mission.*

Divine was back in the news in April 1937, when process servers tried to issue him a summons to appear in court on one of his ongoing cases. Divine fled when he spotted the men, and in the scuffle that followed, one of his followers stabbed a court official. Police began an eight-state search for Father Divine and finally located him in Connecticut. He was arrested and brought back to New York, but was soon released.

Around the same time, one of Father Divine's longtime followers left the movement and published a booklet in which she attacked the preacher. The former follower, Faithful Mary, wrote that Divine was not God, but an ordinary man who unfairly profited from his followers' hard work. Mary also charged that Father Divine had physical relationships with female followers, although such relationships were forbidden.

As Mary's claims made headlines, another former follower was causing trouble for Father Divine. Verinda Brown filed a lawsuit against the preacher, claiming that she and her husband had given

After the death of Penniniah in 1940, Divine married twenty-year-old Edna Rose Ritchings (pictured), one of his Canadian-born followers.

Divine their entire life savings. Now the Browns were trying to get back the $4,476 they felt they were owed. To Father Divine's horror, the judge ruled in the Browns' favor. Divine worried that the ruling would spur other former members to file lawsuits. He immediately appealed the court's decision.

By the end of 1938, Divine and his followers were able to breathe a giant sigh of relief. Faithful Mary came back to the group and retracted her damaging charges, and the Brown case was still tied up in the appeals court. Even so, Father Divine had learned how easily his organization could fall apart, and he took steps to protect the movement from future attacks. For starters, Divine established the Peace Mission as an official church and tried to take greater control over all of its activities.

Divine also created a hierarchy within the church. Near the top of the hierarchy, beneath Father Divine and his wife, was a group of loyal followers who were given special responsibilities in the church. The women, called "Rosebuds" and "Lily Buds," sang in the church choir, while the men, called "Crusaders," served food at Holy Communion banquets. Father Divine hoped this new setup would give some strength and organization to the movement.

Life remained quiet for Father Divine until 1939, when the appeals court in New York sided with Verinda Brown and ordered Divine to pay the $4,476. Father Divine refused to pay the settlement. Instead, he and his wife moved to Philadelphia, where the New York courts had no authority. The Peace Mission Movement would never be the same.

Final Years

Less than a year after moving to Philadelphia, Divine's wife Penniniah passed away. The early 1940s were quiet years for Father Divine. The country had joined World War II, and everyone's attention was on the war effort. Even Divine's fiercest critics seemed too preoccupied to pay him much notice. Although the Peace Mission membership dropped during the war, Father Divine did keep a group of loyal followers.

In 1946 Father Divine married a Canadian-born follower, a twenty-year-old white woman named Edna Rose Ritchings. Divine told his followers that his new wife was really Penniniah, who had always wished to leave her weakened body and be reborn in a more youthful form. Although this was the first time Father Divine had mentioned reincarnation, only a few of his followers doubted his claim. The couple's anniversary, April 29, became a major church holiday.

By the early 1950s, Father Divine had almost completely left the public spotlight. The controversy surrounding his teachings had died down, and the press coverage of his church had slowed to a trickle. In 1953 one of Father Divine's wealthier followers gave him a beautiful seventy-two-acre estate in suburban Philadelphia. The estate, known as Woodmont, included a pool, tennis courts, stream, and enormous mansion. Divine, who was then in his seventies and suffering from diabetes and heart disease,

An aged Father Divine, surrounded by many of his female followers, waves from the porch of his Woodmont estate, which became the focal point of the Universal Peace Mission.

announced he would retire at Woodmont. Because Father Divine could no longer travel, the Universal Peace Mission came to Woodmont. The estate became the center of church life, just as the Sayville, Long Island, home had been so many years earlier. For ten years, Divine preached and held Communion banquets at Woodmont.

On February 10, 1965, Father Divine died at Woodmont after a half century of preaching. Today there are a handful of Peace Missions in several U.S. cities. Members continue Father Divine's tradition of serving lavish Communion banquets—and they leave a place for him at the table.

CHAPTER 4

L. Ron Hubbard: The Church of Scientology

Science fiction readers know the name L. Ron Hubbard. From the 1930s to the 1970s, Hubbard wrote hundreds of sci-fi novels, from extra terrestrial adventures to strange futuristic tales. Several of Hubbard's writings were made into Hollywood films. However, Hubbard's best known creation was his church, Scientology. The Church of Scientology is one of the largest and most powerful new religious movements of the twentieth century; it brought L. Ron Hubbard fame, fortune, and controversy.

Hubbard's Early Years

Lafayette Ronald Hubbard was born on March 11, 1911, to May and Harry Ross Hubbard, a young couple from Omaha, Nebraska. Ron, as his parents nick named him, had bright red hair and a feisty personality. Before Ron's first birthday, the Hubbards moved to Montana, where they were joined by May's family, the Waterburys. The Hubbards and the Waterburys made their home in Helena, a city in the shadow of the Rocky Mountains. Young Ron was surrounded by loving parents, grandparents, and aunts.

For several years, Ron's father hopped from job to job in Helena. But in 1917 the United

L. Ron Hubbard, the science fiction writer who founded the religious movement known as the Church of Scientology.

States entered World War I, and Harry Ross Hubbard enlisted in the navy. When Ron was a sophomore in high school, Harry Ross Hubbard received word that he would be posted in Guam, an island in the Pacific Ocean, far from the battlefields of Europe. Ron's parents decided to bring Ron to Guam for a short vacation, then send him to live with his grandparents in Montana until he completed high school.

Ron enjoyed his first taste of world travel. While sailing toward Guam aboard navy ships, he saw Hawaii, Japan, China, Hong Kong, and the Philippines. Back in Montana, he told everyone who would listen about his adventure. The local newspaper even ran a story about his trip. Those who knew Ron say this experience gave him a taste for travel that would stick with him for life. After returning to Montana and finishing the school year, Ron packed up and left. According to Ron's Aunt Marnie, "[Ron] just got itchy feet. . . . He was an adventurer at heart. The wanderlust was in him and he couldn't see himself staying in a little town like Helena when there was adventure ahead." [16] Ron found a navy ship headed for Guam and hopped aboard.

In Guam, Ron was reunited with his parents. His mother helped him study for college entrance exams, and Ron began to talk about attending the Naval Academy in Annapolis, Maryland. But when the Hubbards returned to the mainland in 1929, Ron learned that he had not been accepted into the academy. He gave up on his plans for a naval career and decided to study civil engineering at George Washington University.

At the university, Ron was once again distracted by adventure. He spent much of his time learning to hang glide and pilot small planes rather than studying. He also found a new passion: writing adventure stories in his journal. Ron finished his first year of college with a D average. When his grades did not improve after his second year at George Washington, he decided not to return for a third. Instead, in 1933, Ron married Polly Grubb, a woman he had met while piloting. Soon the couple was expecting its first child. However, money was tight. Fortunately, he was about to discover a moneymaking talent: writing stories.

Evolution of a Storyteller

Hubbard had always enjoyed writing for his school newspapers. His journal was filled with adventure stories based on his travels in Asia and the Pacific. Now was the perfect time for him to use his writing talents. A new type of magazine—the "pulp"—was flourishing in the United States. The pulps were full of action-packed adventure stories. Costing only a dime apiece, they offered an inexpensive way for Americans to escape the realities of the Great Depression, the time of serious economic troubles that had begun in 1929.

Hubbard began selling his stories to the pulp magazines and became well known among editors for his fast and creative work. He settled his wife and son in the small town of Bremerton, Washington. Soon, the couple had a second child, a daughter. Hubbard himself divided his time between his family's home in Bremerton and New York City, the center of the pulp fiction world. Although the time away from home strained his marriage, Hubbard worked hard and began to see success. In addition to the countless stories he published in magazines, the imaginative storyteller wrote and sold several short adventure novels.

Science Fiction

Around 1938 pulp magazines began to change. Instead of tales about war heroes and adventures at sea, they began to feature stories of aliens and strange futuristic technology. This was the birth of science fiction. Hubbard discovered that he was good at writing science fiction, and he churned out story after story.

By 1941 World War II was raging in Europe, and Hubbard, like many Americans, figured it was only a matter of time before the United States entered the war. Hubbard joined the Naval Reserve and served a four-year stint in the war. Afterward, he did not head home to Bremerton. Instead, he traveled to Los Angeles, California, where he met Sara Elizabeth Northrup. In 1946 he married Sara, although he would not be legally divorced from Polly until 1947.

During this era Hubbard continued to earn a living by writing science fiction. By 1949, however, he was boasting to friends and colleagues that he had discovered a brand-new way of thinking that would change the world. Hubbard claimed that while he was in the war, he had discovered a way for people to overcome all diseases of the body and mind. He called this Dianetics, which he defined as "the science of the mind."

In December 1949 a magazine called *Astounding Science Fiction* announced that Hubbard was preparing an article about Dianetics. Although the complete article would not appear in the magazine until May, John Campbell, the editor, was obviously already impressed with Hubbard's new philosophy. He wrote: "[The philosophy's] power is almost unbelievable; it proves the mind not only can but does rule the body completely."[17] Campbell also told readers that Hubbard's new science would cure diseases and give man perfect memory, even of his own birth.

August WRNY STATION 25 Cents

AMAZING STORIES

HUGO GERNSBACK EDITOR

Stories by
H.G.WELLS
A.HYATT VERRILL
JULIAN HUXLEY

EXPERIMENTER PUBLISHING COMPANY, NEW YORK, PUBLISHERS OF
RADIO NEWS · SCIENCE & INVENTION · RADIO LISTENERS' GUIDE · AMAZING STORIES · SPARE-TIME MONEY MAKING · RADIO PROGRAM WEEKLY

Hubbard became a prolific writer for pulp magazines like Amazing Stories, *which featured science fiction tales about aliens, outer space, and futuristic technologies.*

As readers waited, Hubbard worked furiously on the article and a full-length book on Dianetics. Did he truly believe in his new philosophy? Hubbard's supporters say that he did—and that he was eager to share his revolutionary ideas with the world. But Hubbard's critics believe otherwise. They argue that the sci-fi enthusiast saw Dianetics as a chance to make some real money. As

46

evidence, they cite a remark Hubbard made while speaking to a convention of science fiction writers in late 1949. "Writing for a penny a word is ridiculous," Hubbard told the crowd. "If a man really wanted to make a million dollars, the best way to do it would be to start his own religion." [18]

A Controversial Article and a Best-Selling Book

In spring of 1950 *Astounding Science Fiction* published Hubbard's much-awaited article on Dianetics. Almost simultaneously, Hubbard released a book about his new idea titled, *Dianetics: The Modern Science of Mental Health*. In the publications, Hubbard claimed that Dianetics could cure blindness, mental illness, asthma, and many other ailments. He wrote that the causes of such illnesses were painful memories called *engrams*. For example, a negative experience in early childhood could make a person sick later in life.

According to Dianetics, the secret to getting rid of engrams was a process called auditing, in which a person answered questions posed by a trained Dianetics counselor, or auditor. Through this process, the sick person could erase his or her engrams and become "clear." According to Hubbard, a "clear" person enjoyed good health, a high degree of intelligence, and a perfect memory.

Many people were impressed with these ideas, and for several months it seemed that L. Ron Hubbard had found instant success. *Dianetics* rose quickly to the top of the best-seller list and sold 150,000 copies in its first year. Worried that people would steal his ideas and use Dianetics for their own gain, Hubbard set up a foundation to publicize his new science. Through the foundation, he offered auditing sessions for $25 per hour and expensive training courses that prepared people to become official Dianetics counselors. He allowed these trained counselors to open auditing centers across the country. Although independent, the centers shared their profits with Hubbard.

Hubbard's fortunes began to sour late in 1950. An increasing number of people—including many doctors and journalists—were skeptical of Hubbard's claims and began to speak out against Dianetics. In addition, because of poor money management, the Dianetics organization was not making a profit. In fact, by the middle of 1951 Hubbard was deeply in debt. When a wealthy Dianetics fan from Wichita, Kansas, offered to provide financial support, Hubbard quickly agreed. But the money did not solve the organization's troubles. Hubbard and his trusted Dianetics leaders could not agree on how to manage the foundation, and there was constant fighting within the group. To make matters worse, Hubbard and his second wife began having problems and decided to divorce.

Hubbard's circumstances began to improve later in 1951. That summer, while teaching a Dianetics course in Wichita, he met Mary Sue Whipp—the woman who would soon become his third wife. In March 1952 Hubbard started to recover financially and

Hubbard uses his E-meter to test whether tomatoes can feel pain. Much like a polygraph machine, the device was alleged to be able to read a person's thoughts and emotions.

professionally as well. He organized a meeting of more than seventy Dianetics enthusiasts in a Kansas hotel and announced a new offshoot of Dianetics. He declared that this new version of Dianetics was much more exact than the old version. Its name, Hubbard said, was Scientology.

Scientology

Hubbard coined the word Scientology from a Latin prefix, *scio*, which has connotations of "deep knowing," and a Greek word, *logos*, or word, which when embedded in an English word means "the study of." Thus Hubbard's new philosophy was based on the principle of "knowing how to know."

Although Scientology was rooted in Dianetics, the new philosophy was much more detailed. While Dianetics focused on the body and mind, Scientology focused on the soul, or what Hubbard called the *thetan*. According to Scientology, thetans were immortal beings that traveled through the universe, inhabiting first one body, then another. Hubbard taught that thetans were all knowing and powerful, but that the thetans trapped inside most people had forgotten their supernatural abilities. The aim of Scientology was to restore those abilities through the auditing process.

Hubbard also showed off a new invention designed to perfect the auditing process. It was called the "E-meter." The E-meter looked and worked a little like the polygraph machine used in so-called lie-detector tests. Hubbard claimed his device could read a person's thoughts and emotions.

With the help of the E-meter, Hubbard predicted that people would become "operating thetans" who enjoyed perfect health and knowledge. The result, he claimed, would be a world without problems. He wrote:

> A civilization without insanity, without criminals and without war, where the able can prosper and honest beings can have rights, and where man is free to rise to greater heights, are the aims of Scientology.[19]

Those who joined Hubbard's new movement became known as Scientologists. They were expected to have frequent auditing sessions, to take courses in Scientology, and to help maintain a positive image of Scientology in the press and the public.

Throughout the mid-1950s, Hubbard wrote books and gave lectures to spread information about Scientology. Scientology centers popped up all over the United States, and Hubbard was soon

Hubbard sits at a desk in his elaborate English estate, Saint Hill. He and his family moved to the residence following the success of his newly founded Church of Scientology.

making a profit. In 1954 he founded the first Church of Scientology in Washington, D.C. Although Hubbard had never been particularly religious, classifying his organization as a religion offered him at least two benefits. First, according to U.S. tax laws, a church does not have to pay taxes on its income. Second, because Americans are guaranteed freedom of religion under the Constitution, calling the group a religion helps protect Scientology from its critics.

As the Church of Scientology grew worldwide, the Hubbards and their three children shuttled back and forth between the United States and Europe. By the late 1950s, the family moved to an elegant English estate called Saint Hill, which served as Scientology's new headquarters. During this era, Hubbard taught courses in Scientology but left much of the organization's management to his aides.

Under Attack

Like Dianetics, Scientology had always had its critics. In the early to mid-1960s, those critics became more vocal. In 1963 the U.S. Food and Drug Administration (FDA), the agency responsible for ensuring the safety of food and medicine, raided a Scientology office. The FDA claimed that the church's E-meters were being used as medical devices without the FDA's approval. Hubbard responded by saying that the FDA's raid was an attack on Scientologists' freedom of religion.

Scientology also met resistance outside the United States. In 1965 the government of Victoria, Australia, outlawed Scientology as a dangerous cult. Around the same time, Britain began to investigate Hubbard and his church.

Hubbard did not take these criticisms sitting down. In Australia he simply changed the name of his organization to the Church of New Faith. Worldwide, he urged Scientologists to attack their attackers, to investigate enemies of the church and, if necessary, use the information as fuel for blackmail. Hubbard also found a way to shift attention away from the negative publicity. He announced that a South African man had become the Church of Scientology's first "clear," having successfully erased all his painful memories and achieved perfect health and knowledge.

None of these efforts succeeded for long. When Hubbard continued to meet resistance from governments around the world, he knew it was time for a different kind of response.

The Sea Organization

In 1967 Hubbard moved Scientology's headquarters to a place where it would be safe from governmental interference: the open sea. He purchased a small fleet of ships, handpicked some loyal Scientologists, and named this group the "Sea Organization."

The "Sea Org," as it was nicknamed, sailed the Atlantic Ocean and the Mediterranean Sea. Hubbard called himself the "Commodore" and stayed aboard the main ship, the *Royal Scotsman*, which he eventually renamed the *Apollo*. Onboard this and all the ships, members worked hard, studied Scientology, and faced strict discipline. For example, if a crew member failed to perform a task to Hubbard's satisfaction, the person was attached to a rope and tossed overboard, to spend a while thrashing in the chilly water. As part of this Sea Org tradition, Hubbard or another Scientology officer would recite, "We cast your sins and errors to the waves and hope you will arise a better thetan."[20]

Hubbard docked his ships frequently in Greece, Morocco, and other Mediterranean countries in order to stay in close contact with Scientology offices around the globe. By 1969, their reports troubled him: Scientology continued to face opposition around the world. Within two years, Hubbard's ships were banned from docking in some countries, including Portugal and Greece. In other ports, Hubbard was allowed to dock but was told that neither he nor his crew could leave the ship.

In 1972, while staying in Morocco, Hubbard received word that France was prosecuting the Church of Scientology for defrauding its followers—and that Hubbard might have to stand charges. Because his vessels were docked for the winter, Hubbard could not flee by ship. Instead, he flew to New York City, where he and some assistants stayed hidden in an apartment for almost a year. When the threat died down, Hubbard returned to Europe, organized his fleet, and set sail.

Members of the Sea Org noticed some changes in the "Commodore" on this voyage. Hubbard grew paranoid and distrustful and began to communicate less and less with his crew. Instead, he sent messengers all around the ship to convey his wishes. For example, one messenger might be sent to tell the cook what Hubbard wanted for supper. Another might be sent to order a deckhand to repolish a railing. Hubbard called his messengers the Commodore's Messenger Organization. Some of the messengers were as young as fourteen years old, but they became some of the most trusted—and most powerful—members of the church.

By 1975 Hubbard had grown tired of living aboard the *Apollo*. He decided to scrap the Sea Org and return to the United States. In October Hubbard purchased two buildings in Clearwater, Florida, to serve as Scientology's headquarters. Aware that many of Scientology's critics were on his trail, Hubbard bought the central Florida property in the name of the Southern Land Sales and Development Corporation, a fake business.

The increasingly paranoid Hubbard did not reveal his whereabouts, even to members of the church. His secrecy could not be maintained for long, however. In 1976 reporters learned that Hubbard was staying in Clearwater. Hubbard and two aides hurriedly moved to Washington, D.C. They stayed very close to the Scientology office there but did not let on that they were in town.

The Wrong Side of the Law

For years Hubbard had worried that enemies of Scientology—including former followers, members of the media, and even the

In the late 1970s, Hubbard and two of his aides lived near the Washington, D.C., Scientology office (pictured). At the time, however, Hubbard did not disclose his whereabouts.

U.S. government—were plotting against the church. In the 1960s he had set up the Guardian's Office, a top-secret department within the church whose mission was to keep tabs on all enemies. Convinced that the U.S. government was among the church's enemies, Hubbard had instructed members of the Guardian's Office to take jobs inside the Internal Revenue Service, the Drug Enforcement Agency, and other government agencies. Once inside these agencies, the Scientologists were supposed to copy and steal records related to the church and its enemies. Biographers believe that Hubbard had two goals: to find out what the government knew about Scientology and to get information that could be used to blackmail enemies. Hubbard called this project "Operation Snow White" and put his wife, Mary Sue, in charge of it.

In June 1976 Operation Snow White began to fall apart. FBI agents noticed two Scientologists in the library of a U.S. courthouse, preparing to break into an office. Although the two presented fake IDs and were let go at first, before long, one of the Scientologists was arrested and the other was on the run.

For a while, Ron and Mary Sue seemed to ignore the trouble that was brewing. They bought a million-dollar ranch in La Quinta, California, and moved there in October 1976. However, in July 1977, the Scientologist who had fled from the FBI turned himself in and told about Mary Sue's involvement in the spy operation. In 1979 Mary Sue and eight other Scientologists were charged with stealing government documents, obstructing justice, and other crimes. L. Ron Hubbard insisted he knew nothing about the spy operation and was not charged.

Hubbard's Last Years

In February 1980, while his wife was in prison, L. Ron Hubbard disappeared with two trusted Scientologists. For six years, the trio lived on a ranch in Creston, California. While in hiding, Hubbard wrote his first science fiction book in more than thirty years, an eight-hundred-page novel titled *Battlefield Earth*. Aside from the book, which was published in 1982, the public had little evidence that Hubbard was even still alive.

Hubbard tends to plants in his experimental greenhouse. Today, years after Hubbard's death, thousands of people belong to his Church of Scientology.

On January 24, 1986, at the age of seventy-four, Hubbard died suddenly of a blood clot in the brain. Two days after his death, Hubbard's body was cremated, and his aides scattered the remains in the Pacific Ocean. Because most Scientologists had not known where Hubbard was living, church officials were able to keep the news of Hubbard's death quiet for several days.

Today, the Church of Scientology continues to flourish. With an active membership in the tens of thousands—including celebrities—it is by far L. Ron Hubbard's most lasting legacy.

CHAPTER 5

Sun Myung Moon: The Unification Church

To tens of thousands of faithful followers, the Reverend Sun Myung Moon is the most important person who ever lived. They believe their leader was chosen by God to unite all of humankind in peace and to establish God's heavenly kingdom on earth. In the eyes of his critics, however, Sun Myung Moon is a dangerous fraud. These critics say that Moon's main goal is not a divine kingdom on earth, but a financial and political kingdom of his own. And they claim that for decades, Moon has done whatever was necessary to meet that goal, even brainwashing his followers.

It is hard to say what Moon's true motivation has been. For most of his life, religion, politics, and business have gone hand in hand.

Reverend Sun Myung Moon, the controversial leader of the Unification Church.

Moon's Upbringing

The Reverend Sun Myung Moon was born on January 6, 1920, in Pyungan Buk-do, a small village in northwest Korea. Moon's parents, Moon Kyung-yoo and Kim Kyung-gye, were peasants whose families had farmed the mountainous land for centuries. The couple had eight children, including the serious, quiet Moon. At birth he was given the name Young Myung Moon, which in Korean means "Shining Dragon."

At the time of Moon's birth, Korea was in political and religious upheaval. For more than ten years, the small Asian nation had been a colony of Japan. The Japanese considered the Koreans to be an inferior race and took control of the Koreans' daily lives, forcing them to worship the Japanese emperor as part of the traditional Japanese religion, called Shintoism. In addition, because the Japanese exported and sold most of the rice grown by Korean farmers with little or no compensation to the farmers themselves, many Koreans—especially farmers like the Moons—were living in poverty.

Korea did not have a strong army or a dynamic ruler to fight off the Japanese. For most Koreans, the only means of coping with the oppression was through religion. Despite the Japanese insistence that Koreans adopt the Shinto religion, other faiths continued in secret—including a small but growing Christian presence.

Like many other Korean families, the Moons found strength in their faith. For the first ten years of Moon's life, his family practiced Chinese Confucianism. Then, in 1930, the Moons converted to Presbyterianism, a Christian denomination. The family was heartened by the Presbyterian Church's strong stand against the Japanese occupation of Korea. Growing up, Young Myung Moon took religion very seriously. He was quiet and prayerful. He attended religious schools and later even helped to teach at a Presbyterian Sunday school.

Early Ministry

On Easter morning in 1936, Moon had an experience that changed him forever. He tells that when he was marking this Christian holy day by praying on a mountain near his home, Jesus appeared to him. In this vision, Jesus said that he had been crucified before he could finish his work on earth and that he needed Moon's help to restore earth and humankind to the perfect condition in which God created them. According to Moon, Jesus asked him to prepare God's kingdom on earth, in which people would live together in peace and love.

Moon's writings report the occurrence of similar visions over several years, even as he pursued other interests. In 1938 he traveled to Seoul, Korea, to study electrical engineering. After completing his coursework there, he moved on to Waseda University in Japan to continue his studies. Upon returning to Korea, Moon joined a movement to end the Japanese occupation of Korea. This involvement led to Moon's arrest, and he was jailed for four months. Throughout this time, Moon claims, he frequently communicated with Jesus, Moses, Buddha, and God.

Moon has said that when he was twenty-five years old, God appeared to him once again and told him that he must choose between a life as a minister and a life as an engineer. Remembering his mountaintop encounter, Moon decided to abandon his engineering training and establish a new church. In the mid-1940s, Moon moved to Pyongyang, a city in northern Korea, and founded a small church called Kwang Ya. As he began his preaching, Moon changed his given name from Young to Sun. His new name, Sun Myung Moon, means "Shining Truth."

In addition to starting his church, Moon married and had a son. And in the late 1940s he began recording his revelations from God in a long essay titled *The Divine Principle*. This essay would later become the most important text in Moon's ministry.

According to Moon, Jesus first appeared to him on Easter 1936. In the vision, the messiah asked Moon to finish his divine work on earth.

While Moon was setting up his ministry in Pyongyang and preparing *The Divine Principle*, the world around him was changing rapidly. World War II, which had been raging for several years, ended in 1945. The United States and other Allied forces had defeated Japan and forced Japan to surrender Korea. After the war, Korea was divided, with troops from the communist Soviet Union occupying the north and U.S. troops occupying the south. Moon, who was living in the north, was in a dangerous situation. The communists were atheists and had outlawed the practice of any form of religion in North Korea. Yet Moon continued to lead his growing church and to talk publicly about his divine encounters.

Imprisonment and Freedom

While Moon saw his church as the one, true Christian faith, his ideas were rejected by other Christian churches. The controversial preacher was even banned from the Presbyterian Church of his youth. The Communists were not impressed with Moon's ideas, either. In February 1948 Moon was arrested for "advocating chaos in society" and was sent to the communist-run Hungnam labor camp, where his punishment was to fill hundred-pound bags of fertilizer and load the bags onto railroad cars.

Moon was imprisoned for nearly three years. During that time, Korea's political situation grew even more tumultuous. In 1950 communist North Korea, with the backing of China and the Soviet Union, invaded the south. This resulted in a bloody civil war that killed millions. The United States and other noncommunist countries worked to assist the South Korean troops. In October 1950 these troops helped to liberate Hungnam prison, freeing Moon and other political prisoners.

After being set free, Moon and two of his religious disciples settled in the city of Pusan, South Korea, in January 1951. There, Moon built a small hutlike church and resumed his ministry. During the day, he worked on the docks to earn a living, but at night, he preached to his growing group of followers. While in Pusan, Moon was reunited with his wife, Sungil Choi, and their son. However, the marriage had weakened during the long separation and Sungil Choi did not agree with many of her husband's religious teachings. The couple soon divorced.

In 1953 Moon moved to the bustling capital city of Seoul, South Korea. A year later, he founded the church for which he is famous: the Holy Spirit Association for the Unification of World Christianity—or, simply, the Unification Church.

The Unification Church

Three years after establishing the Unification Church, Moon published his *Divine Principle* in book form. Running almost six hundred pages long, printed in both Korean and English, the volume offers a detailed description of the Unification Church's theology. *The Divine Principle* is based on several main ideas. Some are simple notions of good and evil, and the need for a messiah, or savior, to save earth from sin and restore it to goodness. One idea, however, is unique to the Unification Church: Moon wrote that God originally sent his son, Jesus, to lead people to goodness, but Jesus was killed before he could complete the task by marrying and having a perfect family; now God would send a new savior, who would marry and have children.

Sun Myung Moon said that *he* was the new messiah. He announced that to fulfill his mission, he would marry a "perfect," sinless woman. Together, Moon and his wife would be known as the perfect "True Parents" and their children would be born without sin. This perfect family would be the beginning of God's kingdom.

Moon assured his followers that they, too, could share in God's kingdom by joining the Unification Church and marrying a spouse chosen by Moon. In addition, members of the Unification Church were required to follow some strict rules of behavior. The church did not allow drinking, smoking, or gambling. The church also required members to help spread the Unification Church beliefs.

Before long, Moon's theology began to attract public attention. Many Koreans did not believe in Moon's strange-sounding visions and considered the church an unusual cult. And many of them

Moon and his wife, known as "True Parents," preside over a 1997 mass wedding ceremony. Moon himself arranges the marriages of his devotees.

disapproved when forty-year-old Moon chose a seventeen-year-old girl, Hak Ja Han, as his new wife. Moon claimed that Hak Ja Han was the perfect woman who would help him fulfill his mission. He called her True Mother and named himself True Father.

The following year, Moon began a long tradition of arranging marriages among his followers (arranged marriages were not uncommon in Korea at that time). In 1961, he married the first 36 couples in an elaborate ceremony. He then asked these couples to travel all over Korea, spreading information about the Unification Church. Thanks partly to their aggressive missionary work, the church began to grow steadily throughout South Korea.

Around this time, Moon launched several of his own businesses, including a vitamin company and a pharmaceutical company, and invested heavily in others. Moon's dedicated followers ran the firms efficiently, and the businesses soon became successful. Moon himself became a wealthy man. He and his wife lived in a spacious apartment above the church headquarters in Seoul. They started a family (which would grow to include thirteen children by the 1970s), and enjoyed their elevated status as the "True Family." As the revered leaders of the Unification Church, they were waited on hand and foot by followers.

Worldwide Growth

In the late 1950s and early 1960s, Moon began sending missionaries to other countries. In 1957, a church member named Sang Ik Choi went to Japan and began to recruit new followers, mostly young people in their late teens and twenties. Under Sang Ik Choi's leadership, the Japanese branch of the church was more strict than the main church in Korea. In Japan, followers were expected to live, work, eat, and pray together in one building. This strategy helped to ensure followers' loyalty to Moon and the church.

Before long, the Unification Church also spread to the United States. In 1959, Moon sent a loyal follower, Young Oon Kim, to share the church's teachings among Americans. Kim settled on the West Coast, near the University of Oregon. She attempted to recruit university students to the Unification Church, which she called the "Unified Family," but did not meet with much success.

Although Kim had not found many Americans who were interested in the Unification Church beliefs, her replacement on the West Coast was more successful, and soon hundreds of young Americans were signing up for what they perceived as a life of peace, love, and prayerfulness.

The Reverend Moon in America

By the early 1970s it had become clear to Sun Myung Moon that the Unification Church had potential for growth in the United States. In 1971, after a series of popular speaking tours in this country, Moon decided to move here with his family. Moon told his Korean followers that God had directed him to make the move because America was in moral decline: Americans were being swept up in a sea of drugs, alcohol, and immoral behaviors. According to Moon, only the Unification Church could save the troubled nation.

A "Moonie" listens intently as the Reverend Sun Myung Moon speaks at a massive rally in the United States.

Moon's residence in the United States helped to fuel the church's growth in North America. Between 1972 and 1976 the membership skyrocketed from several hundred to well over six thousand. Soon the Unification Church and the "Moonies," as church members were nicknamed, became household words in the United States. The church was especially known for its aggressive recruitment style. Moon had several tried-and-true techniques for attracting newcomers to his church. One strategy was to give speeches and conduct massive rallies on college campuses and other places where large numbers of young people gathered. Although Moon's speeches were often long and dry, his followers' enthusiasm was contagious.

Another recruitment technique the Moonies used was to approach young people in airports, bus terminals, and city streets. The Moonies looked for a young traveler who seemed to be lost or lonely and invited him or her to attend a church dinner or weekend seminar at one of the Unification Church's communal homes. Sometimes, the Moonies did not reveal the real name of the church until the newcomer was "hooked." According to Nansook Hong, who spent many years in the Unification Church and was married to Moon's eldest son:

61

Brides and grooms line up during a mass wedding ceremony hosted by the Unification Church, which critics believe brainwashes members into blindly obeying church doctrine.

It is a classic church recruitment technique, befriending a young person traveling alone far from home. The conversation is soon steered from pleasantries to philosophy to the church. A successful encounter ends with the tourist agreeing to attend a lecture or meeting. Some of them never go home.[21]

According to some former church members, once a newcomer became involved in the group, he or she grew to be highly dependent on the group and was unlikely to leave. In 1975 a young man named Christopher Edwards was invited by some California Moonies to attend a weekend workshop on a Unification Church farm. The weekend turned into weeks, and the weeks into months. Edwards described his experience this way:

By the end of my third week on the farm, my mind had been swept clean of doubt, a whitewashed wall, a clean tablet to be scribbled upon at will. I confessed my total dependence on the group, which I allowed to regulate all my eating and sleeping habits; they told me when I could and couldn't go to the bathroom, directed me when to pray and when to talk, or be still, when to laugh and when to cry.[22]

Moon and his church members saw nothing wrong with their recruitment efforts and say that reports like Edwards's were greatly exaggerated. When questioned by the press, Moon said that it was the truth of his message that attracted so many people. In one interview he stated, "We talk to people and bring them to hear *The Divine Principle* . . . no doors are locked and anyone can leave anytime from our centers. But people stay to hear the teaching."[23]

Nonetheless, in the 1970s, many Americans were growing suspicious of the Moonies. As more and more teens and young adults joined the church, newspapers began running articles suggesting that young people were being "brainwashed," or mentally tricked, into following Moon. Alarmed parents even hired people to kidnap their children from the church. Although many experts now question whether people can in fact be "brainwashed" into acting against their will, there is little doubt that Moon's recruitment strategies were effective. By 1974 the Unification Church boasted approximately twenty-five thousand American members and many more in 120 countries worldwide.

A Financial Empire

In addition to recruiting new members, the Reverend Moon's followers were expected to raise money for the church. To raise funds, Moonies often stood on street corners selling dried flowers and religious books and tapes. These fund-raising efforts brought in thousands of dollars each week, yet this was only a fraction of the money pouring into the church. Most of Moon's millions came from the many businesses the preacher owned. Based mostly in South Korea, these businesses had been started years earlier with the help of his followers and included hotels, newspapers, even a major vitamin and health food company.

With some of the incoming cash, Moon purchased two mansions in Tarrytown, New York, and established a training center for church leaders there. Moon settled his growing family in one of the Tarrytown estates, but continued to make regular visits to Korea and other nations where his church had a foothold.

Like the Moonies' recruitment techniques, the church's wealth attracted negative attention. Many people believed that Moon was taking advantage of his followers to make himself rich. The negative publicity did not seem to bother Moon, though. In fact, he claimed that criticism simply made his church stronger. In 1977, he stated,

> In a way, I am gratified to have such all-out negative publicity. . . . Every religious pioneer, including Jesus Christ, was persecuted by his contemporaries. . . . But the persecution and hostilities only make our members and me stronger.[24]

Moon's Political Activity

For Moon, the line between religion and politics had always been thin. Since his church's early days in Korea, Moon had used his pulpit to speak out against communism. Now, in the United States, Moon again entrenched himself in politics. Some observers believe Moon had political aspirations of his own, but he never ran for public office. Instead, he took every opportunity to sway the opinions of existing elected officials.

In the early 1970s, for example, Moon publicly supported the U.S. government's decision to keep troops in Vietnam to help the

Moon (left) and an associate give an animated speech. From his powerful pulpit, Moon has been outspoken about his political beliefs.

South Vietnamese fight communists from the north. Moon also raised money and held demonstrations to aid Richard Nixon when the president became the center of the Watergate scandal in 1972. Although Nixon eventually resigned, Moon's work on the president's behalf resulted in a tremendous amount of publicity for the Unification Church and its leader.

To further spread his conservative political beliefs, Moon launched several newspapers, including the *Washington Times*, one of the largest newspapers in the nation's capital. He also financed *Inchon*, a $48-million-dollar Hollywood movie about the Korean War. Moon says that the movie, which glorifies the Korean War and portrays communism in a negative light, reflects God's will.

The Tide Turns

Although Moon had never shunned publicity, he received more attention than he had bargained for in 1982, when he encountered trouble with U.S. tax laws. In that year Moon was charged with failing to report part of his income to the U.S. Internal Revenue Service and with lying on his personal income tax returns. According to the charges, Moon owed hundreds of thousands of dollars in back taxes. Moon pleaded not guilty to the charges and gave outraged speeches in which he called his arrest an example of religious and racial discrimination. He claimed that his enemies were out to destroy the Unification Church.

Many conservative politicians and religious leaders—including the well-known evangelist Jerry Falwell and the nondenominational National Council of Churches—believed that Moon's accusations of bias against him might be justified. Some publicly suggested that Moon was being singled out because of his religious beliefs. Despite this show of support, Moon was convicted in the spring of 1982 and was sentenced to a $25,000 fine and eighteen months in a federal prison. Although Moon appealed the ruling, an appeals court upheld both the conviction and the sentence. In July 1984 Sun Myung Moon entered a federal prison in Connecticut, but he continued to manage the affairs of the Unification Church. He was released in August 1985, after thirteen months.

After his release, Moon continued the Unification Church's recruitment efforts. But negative publicity surrounding Moon's conviction had taken its toll, and U.S. membership in the group steadily declined. Moon faced other difficulties as well. Government investigations put him under great pressure to leave the

Conservative evangelist Jerry Falwell (pictured) was among the religious leaders who spoke out against Moon's arrest and conviction.

United States, and he was losing money in almost all his U.S.-based businesses. In the late 1980s Moon began moving most of the church's personnel and businesses to Asia, where he has focused most of his preaching and business activities for the past fifteen years. Moon has, however, remained the active leader of the U.S. branch of the Unification Church.

A Future in Question

In the late 1990s, as Sun Myung Moon approaches his eightieth birthday, he and his "True Family" continue to lead the Unification Church. He insists—just as he has for nearly forty years—that the Unification Church will one day change the world. As he remarked during a 1998 speech in New York City:

> We cannot expect happiness and a peaceful world without the presence of fundamental changes. The problems of today must be resolved by a True-Parents-centered, True Family ideology.[25]

However, the future of the Unification Church is in question. By 1999 Moon had still not announced any concrete plans for the management of the church after his death. Whomever he chooses will have a significant responsibility. With four thousand members in the United States and many others abroad, Moon's church remains a sizable religious movement. And with businesses and other assets valued at hundreds of millions of dollars, the church is one of the wealthiest religious cults ever established. Moon himself is certainly the world's richest cult leader; when he dies, he will leave behind a personal fortune of several billion dollars.

CHAPTER 6

Jim Jones:
The Peoples Temple

On November 18, 1978, in a small farming commune in South America, more than nine hundred members of a religious cult known as the Peoples Temple died in a mass suicide-murder. News photographs showed Peoples Temple members lying with their faces to the ground, some still holding hands. They were men and women, blacks and whites, infants and grandmothers.

Among the dead was Jim Jones, the forty-seven-year-old leader of the Peoples Temple. In the weeks and months following the tragedy, the public would learn a great deal about Jones. They would learn that he had promised his followers a utopia, or "heaven on earth," in a South American jungle. They would learn that Jones's utopian community, called Jonestown, had been plagued with problems from the start. And, sadly, the public would learn that Jones himself had ordered his faithful followers to their deaths.

Jones's Childhood

James Warren Jones was born on May 13, 1931, in Crete, Indiana. At the time of his birth, Jim's parents, Lynetta and James Thurmond Jones, owned a forty- to sixty-acre farm. However, like many other families across the United States, the Joneses were

Jim Jones, the leader of the Peoples Temple, established a commune with his followers and then called for their mass suicides-murders.

struggling to make ends meet, for the Great Depression was having disastrous effects throughout the nation's economy. In 1934, when Jim was three years old, the Joneses lost their farm. Lynetta and James packed up their only child and moved to Lynn, Indiana, about eighty miles east of Indianapolis.

Despite the move, living conditions did not improve much for the Joneses. The family settled in a poor section of town, and Lynetta Jones worked long hours in a factory to support her family. Jim's father had suffered a lung injury while serving in World War I and rarely worked. Instead, he spent much of his time playing cards at the local pool hall and, according to his son, participating in the Ku Klux Klan, a white supremacist organization founded in the South after the Civil War.

The Makings of a Minister

While growing up in Lynn, Jim had few close friends. He did not play sports or join clubs, and he never really fit in at school. He did, however, show a passion for religion. As a preteen, Jim enjoyed "playing minister" and often pretended to baptize other kids in a creek. He conducted mock funeral services for friends' pets and for dead rats he found in the street.

Young Jim also began to explore various religions. Although the senior Joneses were not particularly religious, Jim attended church services with neighbors. Through such services, Jim was exposed to Pentecostalism, an intensely emotional form of Christianity. Pentecostal Christians believe that the truly faithful acquire the ability to speak in tongues, or mysterious languages, and that through faith a person can be instantly cured of physical diseases. Pentecostal services are often characterized by enthusiastic singing and shouting. Jim was impressed with what he saw. As one biographer writes:

> The Pentecostalists were Jim's favorites. In that setting of warmth and freedom of emotion where people hugged and praised Christ, Jim Jones experienced the delicious taste of acceptance for the first time in his life.[26]

It is not surprising, then, that Pentecostal ideas and practices would later influence Jones's own teachings.

During his adolescence, Jones also began studying the works of Karl Marx and other socialist philosophers. These philosophers described an ideology based on equality, social justice, and cooperation. They envisioned a world in which individuals would not own property or pursue wealth for themselves, but would work together for the good of the community. These ideas, like Pentecostalism, had a great impact on Jones.

In 1949, after graduating from high school, Jones enrolled at Indiana University and married Marceline Baldwin. In 1951 the couple moved to Indianapolis in order for Jim to continue his studies at Butler University. He enrolled in education courses, thinking that he might become a high school teacher. But Jones's true passion remained religion, and it was not long before he once again felt the urge to preach.

The ideology of German philosopher Karl Marx (pictured) influenced Jones's own beliefs.

Jones began delivering sermons to churches in poor neighborhoods, black as well as white. In 1952 Jones read that the Methodist Church (to which his wife already belonged) had a reputation for combating racism and poverty, and he decided to join. Later that year, he was appointed a student pastor at the Somerset Methodist Church in Indianapolis. This position was intended to be an apprenticeship, or "on-the-job training." But Jones required little training. He was already delivering rousing sermons that filled the church pews.

Formation of the Peoples Temple

Before long, Jones grew unhappy with Methodism. He saw himself as a leader, not a joiner, and he wanted to build a following of his own. In 1954 he left the Methodist Church and formed a new church called Community Unity. The church was small at first, with only about 150 members, but an opportunity for growth was not far away. In September 1954 Jones was invited to speak at the Laurel Street Tabernacle, a Pentecostal church in Indianapolis. He gave several sermons there and performed a variety of phony healings that impressed the congregation. According to former church officials, Jones would hold up a rotting animal organ and claim it was a cancerous growth he had banished from the body or a person Jones had identified as having cancer.

Jones's "healings" attracted large crowds and sizable donations. Church officials even began to consider the popular preacher as a replacement for the pastor, who was planning to retire. But there was a problem. Each time Jones spoke, a number of African Americans showed up for services. That did not sit well with leaders of the all-white church. As one scholar notes:

> At a time when church segregation in the United States was practically total, the guest preacher had brought Blacks to the service, and they had not sat just in the back pews. Seeing the need, the board offered to help establish a separate church for blacks. Jones was outraged by the proposal. "There will be no church in the Black neighborhood," he said. "I will not be a pastor of a Black Church or a White Church. Wherever I have a church, all people will be welcome." Then he walked out.[27]

When Jones walked out, about a hundred people—more than half of the congregation—walked out with him and joined Community Unity. Within two years, Jones had renamed his church to the Peoples Temple Full Gospel Church.

The Peoples Temple was based on the pursuit of equality and social justice and on Pentecostal faith healing. For Jones, the more important of these two missions was working for equality. He claimed to have great concern for people he considered the outcasts of society, especially African Americans. Many people—black and white—felt stirred to join Jones in his struggle. By the late 1950s the Peoples Temple was 20 percent African American and was one of the few interracial congregations in Indiana.

Taking Greater Control

Jones did not simply preach about social justice and equality; he put his words into action. The socialist ideas that had fascinated Jones as a teenager had become a cornerstone of his church, and he established a soup kitchen for the hungry and a system for distributing clothing to the poor. Jones called his approach *apostolic socialism*, by which he meant a religion-based sharing of wealth and goods.

Although Jones knew that his social message would not appeal to everyone, he recognized that his "miracle cures" were an effective way to attract new members. According to former church members, Jones continued the fraudulent faith healings in the hope that once newcomers were drawn in, they would see the value of his social message.

Around 1956 Jones traveled to Philadelphia to meet religious leader Father Divine. The trip seemed to inspire Jones to make changes in the Peoples Temple, and he soon began to take greater control of his followers' lives. For example, he began encouraging his followers to call him "father" or "dad." He asked them to increase their donations to the Peoples Temple. He urged them to spend less time with family and more time at church. Jones told his followers that if they would give up their money and belongings, he would meet all their needs. Many of his followers were happy to comply.

The Rainbow Family

As Jones's church family grew, so did his family at home. Between 1953 and 1959, Jones and his wife adopted four children, including three Korean children orphaned in the Korean War. In 1959

Jones meets with members of the Peoples Temple. In exchange for giving up their money and belongings, Jones promised to take care of all of his followers' needs.

Marceline gave birth to the couple's biological son, Stephan. And in 1961, the Joneses took what was considered a radical step. They adopted Jim Jones Jr., an African-American baby. In doing so, they became the first white couple in Indianapolis to adopt a black child. Jim and Marceline proudly called their brood the "Rainbow Family."

Jones received a great deal of public attention for his multiracial family and church. In 1961 that attention helped him win a position as head of the city's Human Rights Commission, the agency responsible for making sure all citizens in Indianapolis were treated equally regardless of race, age, or gender. Jones often used his position as an opportunity to speak about his church, which now had about five hundred members.

A Long-Range Plan

The early 1960s were a turning point for Jones and the Peoples Temple. Around this time, Jones had a vision that a nuclear bomb would strike Indiana. He became obsessed with this possibility and told his followers that he planned to find a place where the Peoples Temple would be safe. In 1962 Jones left his associate pastors in charge of the Peoples Temple and took his family around the world: first to Hawaii, then to Brazil and several other spots in South America. In 1964 he returned to Indiana.

Back in Indianapolis, the Peoples Temple continued to attract attention—not all of it positive. Because of their radical ideas about race and equality, Jones and his followers received many threats. In 1965 Jones shared with his followers another vision: This time, he told them, the temple must move to Ukiah, California, a quiet logging area in the northern part of the state. An interracial group of about seventy headed west with Jones. Jones told them he had chosen the remote area as a safe haven from both bigotry and nuclear bombs, citing an article in *Esquire* magazine that described this section of California as one of the safest places to be in case of nuclear war. But religious scholars have suggested a possible additional reason for the move:

> Jones also envisioned a unifying experience. . . . Removing his people from their midwestern roots, having them sell their homes and quit their jobs, would make them more dependent, and thus more receptive to total commitment.[28]

Jones believed that such "total commitment" would make the Peoples Temple stronger and his followers less likely to question their faith.

The California Years

The Peoples Temple operated out of California for about ten years. This period was marked by growth, increased public attention, and the first hints that the leader of the Peoples Temple was mentally unstable.

Growth came slowly at first; after two years in California, the group still had only 106 members. But Jones was not discouraged. He took a job teaching night classes to adults and managed to recruit some of his young, white, middle-class students to the Peoples Temple. For four years the members of the congregation met in garages, fairgrounds, and rented buildings. In 1969 they finally built a brand-new church of their own. Then, in the early 1970s, the Peoples Temple added branches in San Francisco and Los Angeles, and membership began to skyrocket. Most of the new urban members were African Americans.

As his congregation grew, Jones set up a hierarchy within his church. At the top of the hierarchy were eight to ten trusted staff members who helped Jones with important decisions. All were young white women. Jones also established the church's Planning Commission, a small group of aides who made sure followers obeyed Jones's many rules. For example, the Planning Commission regulated where members could live and whom they could marry. This was one tool Jones used to control his followers' lives. In addition, the leader demanded that followers give their money to the temple.

Such control tactics forced Jones's followers to grow increasingly dependent on him. Perhaps to encourage this dependency, Jones urged people to throw away their Bibles and stop worshiping the Christian god, which he called the "sky god." He began calling himself "god" and reminded his followers of all he had done for them. At one faith-healing service, he exclaimed:

> What's your sky god ever done? You've asked and begged and pleaded for help with your suffering. And he never gave you any food, he never gave you a home. But I, the socialist worker god, have given you all these things.[29]

During his years in California, Jones became paranoid and distrustful. He worried constantly about being betrayed by his flock. To encourage loyalty, he punished those who broke temple rules with beatings and public lectures. According to former cult members, Jones began to test his followers' loyalty with suicide drills, which he called "White Nights." At each drill, Jones gave his followers drinks that he said had been poisoned. After watching to see who would take the drinks, Jones would announce that there was no poison, that the ordeal had been a test of his followers' faith.

Despite these disturbing developments inside the Peoples Temple, in the outside world, Jones and the temple were still well regarded. Just as he had done in Indianapolis, Jones reached out to the community with good works, establishing homes for the

A curious outsider peers through the elaborate gates of the Peoples Temple branch located in San Francisco.

elderly and a camp for disabled children. He continued to speak out against racism and, in 1975, was named San Francisco's "Humanitarian of the Year." Jones and the temple were also very politically active. They demonstrated against the Vietnam War and rallied to elect George Moscone mayor of San Francisco. After Moscone won the election, he appointed Jones to a high-profile position in the city's Housing Commission.

Jonestown

In 1974 Jones began preparing to move the Peoples Temple out of the United States. He leased more than thirty-eight hundred acres of land in Guyana, the small South American country that lies just east of Venezuela. Guyana had a socialist government, and Jones felt that this made the country a good place to relocate his church. The land he leased was in the middle of the dense Amazon rain forest, but Jones had a plan. He sent a group of young Peoples Temple members to Guyana as "pioneers." These members began clearing the forest and building the Peoples Temple Agricultural Mission, a small farming community that the Guyanese locals called "Jonestown." Jones himself remained in California.

Former temple member Debbie Layton was one of the first to arrive in Guyana. Although she and her fellow pioneers had to work hard to set up the agricultural mission, Layton described those early years as happy ones. In a 1998 interview, she recalled, "When the first pioneers from the [San Francisco] Bay area came down here, they loved it. They cleared the land and they built the cabins and they lived as village people." [30]

While the pioneers built homes and planted crops, Jones began to face serious troubles back in California. Word of the church's strict rules began to surface, along with reports that Jones was having sexual relationships with church members. In 1977 the U.S. Internal Revenue Service noticed the Peoples Temple's political activity and began to question whether the temple was a church that deserved its tax-exempt status or a political organization that should be paying taxes. Jones knew that the outcome of the tax agency's investigation could cost him a great deal of money. For Jones, the final straw was a 1977 article in *New West* magazine that exposed the church's dark secrets—the beatings, the suicide drills—to a wide audience. The writer, San Francisco reporter Marshall Kilduff, had based his report on interviews with former Peoples Temple members. With that article, Jones's public image as a caring social leader was shattered. In July 1977 he de-

A shrub now grows in the abandoned Jonestown pavilion where Jim Jones preached to members of his Peoples Temple church.

cided that it was time to leave the United States altogether. Of the roughly three thousand followers he told to leave with him for Jonestown, almost seven hundred complied.

Descriptions of the conditions in Jonestown after Jones's arrival vary. According to some accounts, the farming commune where Debbie Layton and others had been so content began to resemble a labor camp. Jones placed guards around the settlement and ordered members to work in the scorching-hot fields for up to eleven hours a day. Evenings were reserved for long church meetings. Jones installed loudspeakers throughout Jonestown and broadcast his voice day and night, telling listeners that all outsiders were enemies.

Most church members slept in dormitories and ate mostly rice, vegetables, and milk. Temple members who dared to complain or disobey Jones's orders were punished. Children who misbehaved were reportedly taken out at night and beaten upside down over a snake-filled well. These beatings were broadcast via loudspeaker as a warning to everyone in Jonestown. In addition, young and old alike were subjected to frequent "White Night" suicide drills.

Not everyone paints such a harsh picture of Jonestown. Some former members say that reports of abuses were exaggerated. They remember enjoying the hard work and sense of community. They point out that Jones provided a school and day care center for temple children and medical care for everyone. "For the majority of the members, life in Jonestown was probably a step up from their impoverished lives in the United States. The Peoples Temple group was like a large extended family," says Dr. J. Gordon Melton, an expert on the Peoples Temple and other religious movements.[31] Indeed, more followers left the U.S. for Jonestown.

The Beginning of the End

Whatever the truth, conditions in Jonestown worsened in the summer of 1978. Around that time, Jim Jones started using drugs heavily, including painkillers, tranquilizers, and amphetamines. He claimed to suffer from cancer, heart disease, fevers, a fungus, and other illnesses. Visitors to Jonestown around this time reported that Jones was hardly able to walk on his own. Perhaps because of one of these physical illnesses—or perhaps because of mental illness or drugs—Jim Jones grew increasingly paranoid. Former members recall that Jones began to talk more and more of a threat from the outside world.

In 1978 the enemy that Jones feared appeared. In that year, the attorney for the Peoples Temple, Tim Stoen, left the church and returned to the United States. He and his wife, Grace, joined other people who had left the temple in telling about the mistreatment they had undergone. Stoen had an especially terrible story. He and Grace had been forced to leave their young son, John Victor, behind in Jonestown. Jim Jones claimed that John Victor was actually his own biological son.

The Stoens joined the Concerned Relatives, a group made up of the families of Peoples Temple members. The group, which had first formed in the early 1970s, worried that some temple members were being held against their will. The Concerned Relatives persuaded a U.S. lawmaker, California congressman Leo Ryan, to visit Jonestown. Jim Jones reluctantly agreed to allow Ryan to enter the compound and interview members.

Ryan flew to Guyana, arriving in Port Kaituma on November 14, 1978, along with a handful of aides, fourteen Concerned Relatives, and several journalists. When the group arrived in Jonestown three days later, they were surprised. Despite the horrible reports that had come out of Jonestown, the visitors saw a clean, organized, and apparently happy community. A band played, and temple members danced and sang. Elaborate meals were served. And the first few members with whom Ryan spoke assured him that they were content.

Then, one by one, nearly twenty temple members quietly approached Ryan and his crew to ask for assistance in leaving Jonestown. The next day, November 18, Ryan had a frightening experience that gave him further cause for concern. A temple member rushed at him with a knife, attempting to cut his throat. Although he was not hurt, Ryan decided to cut his visit short. To Jones's displeasure, several temple members decided to return with Ryan to the United States.

The group rode back to Port Kaituma, where two planes were waiting. As the group began to board the planes, a Jonestown tractor appeared on the airstrip. Suddenly, temple guards on the tractor opened fire on Ryan and his crew. After several minutes of gunfire, Congressman Ryan, three journalists, and one Jonestown defector were dead. Others lay injured on the airstrip or fled into hiding in the jungle.

The Tragedy

Back in Jonestown, preparations were already under way for a tragedy of a different kind. "Alert! Alert! Alert!"[32] Jones cried over the loudspeakers. He ordered his followers to assemble in the main pavilion, which was surrounded with armed guards. There, Jones announced that Ryan's visit had confirmed his worst fears. The outside world, he said, would never leave the Peoples Temple alone. Jones informed his followers that they had no choice but to take their own lives. And this time, it was no drill.

Jones's aides prepared a large vat of a grape-flavored drink mixed with potassium cyanide—a deadly poison. They placed the vat in the pavilion. Historians know much of what happened next, for Jones had tucked a tape recorder beneath his chair in the pavilion. First, Jones assigned nurses and parents the task of killing those who were too young to kill themselves. Infants and small children were force-fed or injected with the poison. When children spat out the bitter-tasting mixture, Jones ordered them to remain

The bodies of Peoples Temple members are scattered across the Jonestown commune. Members died after ingesting a poisoned grape drink.

In the aftermath of the Jonestown tragedy, 914 of Jones's followers were dead. Those temple members who could not, or refused to, commit suicide were murdered by their peers.

calm. "Keep your emotions down. Keep your emotions down. Children, it will not hurt. If you'd be—if you'll be quiet," [33] he said.

Then, at Jones's orders, adult members stood in line to drink the deadly concoction. One by one, they sipped the poison, then lay down to die. Throughout the ordeal, Jones repeated his message that suicide was the only escape: "I tell you I don't care how many screams you hear, I don't care how many anguished cries. Death is a million times preferable to ten more days of this life." [34]

In the end, 914 temple members, including 276 children, died in the murder-suicide. A few members managed to survive by fleeing into the forest; one woman, who never left her dormitory, slept through the massacre. Two of Jones's own sons lived because they were at a basketball tournament in another part of Guyana. But these individuals are exceptions; almost all the residents of Jonestown perished that night. Examinations of the bodies later suggested—but did not prove—that not all the temple adults willingly drank the poison; some may have been held down and injected. Autopsy results also showed that Jones himself did not drink the poison. He died instead of a gunshot wound to the head. To this day, no one knows whether the wound was self-inflicted; the tape recordings do not provide an answer.

CHAPTER 7

David Koresh: The Branch Davidians

In late winter of 1993, a dramatic showdown unfolded in a rural area near Waco, Texas. The clash was between one hundred members of a religious sect known as the Branch Davidians, who were barricaded inside their compound, and four hundred law enforcement officials who were stationed outside. The clash began with an exchange of bullets on February 28 and ended fifty-one days later when a deadly blaze engulfed the Davidian compound.

Most major television networks covered the conflict from beginning to end, and millions of viewers tuned in each day. Before long, a single name dominated the nightly news and the public spotlight: David Koresh. Koresh had a long history with the Branch Davidians and had led the group for five years. He died in the inferno that ended the famous standoff. But his story begins thirty-four years earlier, in another Texas town.

David Koresh would become the charismatic leader of the Branch Davidians, a militant religious cult based in Waco, Texas.

Koresh's Childhood

The man known as David Koresh was born Vernon Wayne Howell in Houston, Texas, on August 17, 1959. His parents, Bonnie Clark and Bobby Howell, were unmarried and stayed together only a few years after Vernon's birth. When the couple parted ways, Bonnie, who was only fifteen years old when her son was born, asked her own mother, Erline Clark, to care for young Vernon.

At the age of six, Vernon returned to the custody of his mother, who had since married and moved to Dallas. Vernon started school in Dallas, but a learning disability called dyslexia made it hard for him to read and write. Despite his difficulties at school, Vernon was curious and good at fixing things. He loved animals and made friends easily.

However, Vernon's main interest was religion. He memorized Bible passages and attended a Seventh-Day Adventist church with his mother. This well-known Christian church gets its name from its celebration of the Sabbath, or day of worship, on Saturday, the seventh day of the week. Seventh-Day Adventists also look forward to the Second Advent, or the second coming of Christ. The church became an important part of young Vernon's life. As one biographer notes:

> God and the Bible had dominated [Vernon's] interests since he was a little boy. His mother often watched him return home from school and drop to his knees beside his bed, where he lapsed into fervent prayer. Sometimes he went to the barn to pray in private, and he would remain there for hours in earnest communion with the Lord while tears ran down his cheeks.[35]

As Howell entered high school, his learning problems continued. He dropped out of school at the end of ninth grade and for several years supported himself with odd jobs. He worked briefly as a gas station attendant, carpenter, and landscaper. He even tried to earn money playing his guitar in local clubs.

In 1979, at the age of twenty, Howell was officially baptized into the Seventh-Day Adventist Church in Tyler, Texas. However, by now Howell had spent countless hours memorizing and reflecting on the Bible, and some of his interpretations did not match those of the Seventh-Day Adventists. He began to argue with others in the congregation over church teachings. And when Howell expressed a romantic interest in the pastor's daughter, the pastor told him that he was a bad influence on the young people in the congregation and asked him to leave.

Howell left Tyler and decided to take another stab at playing guitar for a living. He played in several rock and roll bands in Texas and California and even recorded a song. Yet he continued to seek religious fulfillment. In 1981 he discovered a group whose interpretations of the Bible closely matched his own. The group, known as the Branch Davidians, was based near Waco, a small city in east central Texas. The Davidians lived together

The Branch Davidians, an offshoot of the Seventh-Day Adventists, were named after the Biblical king David (pictured).

in a collection of buildings they called Mount Carmel. Twenty-two-year-old Howell joined the group and moved into Mount Carmel.

The Branch Davidians

The Branch Davidians could trace their roots to Howell's child-hood church, the Seventh-Day Adventists. However, the Branch Davidians had broken away from the Seventh-Day Adventists over a period of four decades. In the late 1930s, a Seventh-Day Adventist named Victor Houteff announced that he was a prophet, or messenger of God, who had been selected to reform the church. Houteff left the Seventh-Day Adventists, taking a dozen families with him. He named his small group the Davidians, after the biblical King David, and settled his group near Waco. Houteff predicted the second coming of Christ would happen in 1943, but that year came and went, marked mainly by the continned fighting of World War II.

Houteff managed to hold the Davidians together until his death in 1955, and his wife led the group until 1959, when an energetic new leader named Benjamin Roden took over. Roden renamed the group the Branch Davidians and led them until his death in 1978, when his wife, Lois, assumed leadership of the group. Lois was still the head of the Branch Davidians in 1981, when Howell encountered the sect. Most of the Branch Davidians assumed that Lois's and Benjamin's son, George, would take over the Mount Carmel group after her death. However, Howell would soon have very different ideas.

Howell the Prophet

Howell impressed many Branch Davidians with his knowledge of the Bible, and before long he became an important figure at Mount Carmel. Many Davidians began to view Howell as a prophet of God. Howell also became very close to Lois Roden and, according to many reports, had a brief love affair with her. Howell's timing could not have been better. Lois Roden and her son had had a disagreement, and Lois was beginning to reconsider her assumption that George would one day take over Mount Carmel's leadership. Vernon Howell—a knowledgable, dynamic young man—began to seem like a better choice.

It was no secret that both Vernon Howell and George Roden wanted to lead the Branch Davidians someday. Because almost all the sect members sided with one man or the other, life at Mount Carmel grew tense. Soon the rivalry would come to a head.

In January 1984 Howell married Rachel Jones, the fourteen-year-old daughter of a longtime Branch Davidian. A year later, he and Rachel, now pregnant with the couple's son, traveled to Israel. Howell's absence made it easier for George Roden to win the support of Mount Carmel's residents, and when Lois Roden died in 1986, George ordered Howell to leave Mount Carmel.

Howell left, but he took forty loyal followers with him. Together, they established a new Branch Davidian community on twenty wooded acres near Palestine, Texas. The members lived in shacks and abandoned school buses strewn across the property.

In this new community, Howell's faithful supporters discovered that Howell had returned from Israel with a new message.

Howell now claimed that Jesus would not return for a second coming. Instead, God would send a different "messiah," or savior. Howell, a persuasive speaker who endlessly quoted Scripture, convinced his followers that *he* was that messiah. Howell also said that God had given him the ability to interpret the entire Bible, including the mysterious final chapters called Revelation, which talk about the end of the world. Although Howell failed to announce the exact date at which the world would end, he hinted that it would be in the followers' lifetimes. Howell claimed that, as messiah, he would play an important role when the end came. He described himself as the messenger who "would appear in the last times and reveal the mysteries of God." [36]

Howell also informed his followers that it was his religious duty to have more than one wife. He remained legally married to Rachel but began "marrying" other young Branch Davidian women. He would eventually have at least five wives, many of them in their early teens.

Battle for Leadership

Howell had not seen the last of his rival, George Roden. In November 1987 Roden challenged Howell to a strange contest. Roden said he would dig up the coffin of Anna Hughes, a Branch Davidian who had been dead for twenty years. Whichever man

In a scene from Revelation, the mysterious final chapters of the Bible, the Lord's angels cast fire and destruction upon the earth. Howell claimed that God had granted him the ability to foresee the end of the world.

could raise Hughes from the dead, Roden claimed, was the true Branch Davidian leader.

Howell informed police of Roden's plan but was told he lacked proof that a crime was being committed. With seven followers, an armed Howell sneaked onto Mount Carmel to photograph Hughes's remains, as proof that George was breaking the law by mistreating a corpse. However, Howell was discovered and a gun battle ensued. Howell and his followers were arrested and charged with attempted murder, but were released on bail. Howell then acquired legal claim to the Mount Carmel complex by moving back in and paying property taxes that were overdue. Roden, whose increasingly bizarre behavior had landed him in prison, had not been able to prevent the takeover.

In April 1988 Howell and his seven followers were tried. The jurors found the followers not guilty of attempted murder but were unable to reach a verdict on Howell. The judge finally declared a mistrial, and Howell was free to go. Six months later, George Roden was sent to a facility for the mentally ill. Now Howell's longtime rival was permanently out of the picture.

Back at Waco

After his return to Mount Carmel, Howell began to fix up the rundown seventy-seven-acre property. Through winter and spring of 1989, dozens of followers worked to reinforce the sagging buildings and construct tunnels and passageways linking the community's buildings.

Howell also instituted some strict new rules at Mount Carmel. In 1989 he announced a policy he called the "New Light." According to New Light rules, there were to be no romantic relationships among the Branch Davidians. Even married couples had to live apart. Howell explained that relationships with members of the opposite sex would get in the way of religious studies. Besides, he noted, husbands and wives would be unnecessary in the kingdom of God. The New Light rules, however, did not apply to Howell himself, for he continued to marry and have sex. By the early 1990s, he had fathered twelve children with several Branch Davidian women. Howell claimed that his own wives and children would have a special place in God's kingdom.

"New Light" was not the only rule Howell instituted. He also controlled conditions at the compound—deciding everything from what the Davidians ate to when they slept. For example, Howell insisted that followers rise early each morning and run a military-style obstacle course. Although some Branch Davidians were

A young woman wears a shirt with a picture of David Koresh as she attends a third anniversary memorial service at the Branch Davidian compound in Waco, Texas, on Friday, April 19, 1996.

allowed to leave Mount Carmel to work, most remained at the compound to prepare meals and maintain the property. The Davidians usually shared meals of bread, fruit, milk, salad, and other simple foods. Occasionally, Howell would buy large quantities of takeout food for his flock.

Worship was the most important aspect of life at Mount Carmel. Howell expected his followers to attend daily Bible study sessions, which often ran late into the night. He frequently reminded his followers that only he had the ability to understand and explain the Scriptures.

In many respects besides romantic relationships, the rules that governed the Branch Davidians' lives did not apply to Howell himself. Unlike his followers' modest quarters, Howell's own apartment had television and air conditioning. Howell ate whatever he wanted and was the only Davidian allowed to drink beer. A few followers questioned Howell's inconsistent policies and left the sect. Most accepted Howell's rules because they truly believed that he was the messiah.

Introducing David Koresh

In the summer of 1990 Howell took a step that would help to further cement his authority among the Branch Davidians. He legally changed his name to David Koresh. The first name, David, referred to the biblical king. The surname Koresh is Hebrew for Cyrus, another ancient king. Cyrus is also another word for Christ, or messiah. Howell's powerful new name reinforced his claim that he was chosen by God.

Throughout the late 1980s and early 1990s, Koresh recruited new members. In the United States, he focused his efforts on Texas, California, and Hawaii. Internationally, he concentrated on Canada, England, Australia, New Zealand, Israel, and the Caribbean. Since the Branch Davidians shared a few basic beliefs with the Seventh-Day Adventist Church from which they had evolved, Koresh often aimed his recruitment efforts at members of the longer established group. Like the existing members, most new Branch Davidians were expected to live communally with the rest of the sect. They signed over their savings and pensions to Koresh, and began to share in the Branch Davidian way of life.

Although the Davidians' style of living may have seemed strange to some outsiders, Koresh and his group maintained polite, friendly relationships with the local people. The Davidians kept their property neat and even gave a hand when a neighboring farmer needed help at harvest time. One journalist noted:

> To farmers and tradesmen in the Waco area, Koresh was precise, peaceable, and well-versed in the details of their trade. . . . Koresh could talk Sheetrock, livestock maintenance, field rotation and turbos with anyone.[37]

By most accounts, Koresh and his followers led an unusual but quiet existence. That began to change around 1990, when Koresh started talking more and more frequently and fervently about the approach of the end of the world, an event he felt would be marked by a battle between good and evil. Some former Branch Davidians say that Koresh even began to prepare for this event, which he and the other Davidians called the Apocalypse. According to these reports, Koresh began to stockpile a huge arsenal of weapons, including shotguns, semiautomatic rifles, and ammunition. The reports also claim that Koresh began storing powdered milk, freeze-dried meals, canned foods, and other nonperishable items that would be useful in an emergency. Some media reports say that Koresh gave Mount Carmel a new name: Ranch Apocalypse.

The Clash Begins

By the late 1980s the Branch Davidians had begun to lose members. Some of those who left the group were opposed to the New Light policy banning marriage or did not enjoy the Davidians' strict communal living. But others were alarmed by Koresh's growing collection of weapons and his apparent preference for "marrying" young teenagers. In 1990 some former members living in Australia banded together and hired a detective to study the Branch Davidians. The detective's research confirmed that Koresh had a large quantity of weapons (which Koresh claimed he purchased to resell at gun shows). He also believed that Koresh was sleeping with underage girls and possibly beating other children in

A gun enthusiast fires a semiautomatic rifle at a shooting range. Koresh and his Branch Davidians were allegedly stockpiling such weapons, as well as a supply of ammunition.

the compound. However, he could not prove his shocking charges, and, without more evidence, there was little law officials could do.

In 1992 Koresh's neighbors began to complain that the previously quiet Davidians had become quite noisy. Neighbors frequently heard gunfire and small explosions coming from Mount Carmel. Soon, the federal Bureau of Alcohol, Tobacco, and Firearms, whose responsibilities include enforcing laws related to guns and other firearms, began looking into the case.

ATF, as the bureau is known, learned that Koresh may have broken several gun laws. Although it is not illegal for private individuals to have many, many firearms, Koresh may have illegally altered some of his rifles to turn them into more powerful rapid-fire weapons. The ATF quickly prepared warrants that would enable them to search Mount Carmel and possibly arrest Koresh.

At 7:30 A.M. on Sunday, February 28, 1993, a long line of government vehicles pulled up to Mount Carmel. Just after 9 A.M., ATF agents rushed to the front door of the compound. In a split second, a hail of bullets filled the air. Who fired the first shot is a mystery; but, by the time a cease-fire had been arranged, the raid had exacted a deadly toll. Four ATF agents and six Branch Davidians lay dead, and twenty-four other participants were injured, including Koresh himself.

The cease-fire halted the day's shooting but failed to resolve the larger situation. Instead, it was the beginning of a long standoff.

The Standoff Begins

Late on February 28, the FBI arrived in Waco and took charge. That night, Koresh requested an opportunity to publicly present his side of the situation, and the FBI agreed. Koresh was interviewed on a local religious radio station and on the Cable News Network, a major international television network. In his interviews, Koresh promised to come out on March 2. But first, he said, the radio station would have to play an hour-long taped message from Koresh. The radio station aired the tape Koresh had created, and March 2 came and went, but Koresh did not emerge. He did, however, send a few adults and several children to join some other children who had been sent away from the ranch after the cease-fire of February 28.

To most listeners, including the FBI agents, Koresh's long taped message was almost impossible to understand. The cult leader spoke entirely in biblical language and seemed to make little sense. However, religious scholars who understood the biblical references say that Koresh was explaining why he did not feel ready to surrender to the federal agents. According to these scholars, Koresh and his followers viewed the government raid as an attack on a messenger of God. Koresh, they said, would not come out until he had received a signal from God.

As the days passed with no sign that Koresh was ready to surrender, the FBI began to mount more pressure. In an effort to force the Davidians out, the agents disconnected the electricity at Mount Carmel and began shining bright searchlights on the property all night long. The FBI also blared loud recordings of dental drills, whining rabbits, and other unpleasant sounds. None of these tactics induced Koresh to leave Mount Carmel.

Inside the compound, the Branch Davidians did their best to ignore the annoying lights and sounds. On April 14 Koresh sent out a letter to his lawyer, Dick DuGuerin. The letter stated that Koresh had prayed to God for direction and had been told to record his full interpretation of Revelation. This had to be done, Koresh claimed, before he or his followers could leave Mount Carmel.

The FBI saw Koresh's letter as a delaying tactic and doubted that Koresh really intended to produce the document, even after April 16, when Koresh reported that he had finished the first part of his writing. As researchers point out, this view of Koresh spread quickly among government agents, the media, and the general public: "The official opinion was now fixed: Koresh was a determined, hardened, manipulative, and paranoid adversary who had no intention of delivering himself." [38]

The Standoff Ends

On April 19 the fifty-one-day standoff came to an end. Just before 6 A.M., the FBI telephoned Mount Carmel to inform Koresh that a tear gas attack would begin if the group did not exit the compound soon. Koresh, who believed he was keeping his word to the agents by working on the draft of his biblical interpretation, grew angry and again refused to leave. Instead, he threw the telephone out the window and distributed gas masks and weapons to his followers. At noon, with the Davidians huddled inside the compound, a tank rammed the kitchen storage area, ripping out pieces of the compound's walls and spraying tear gas inside. Other combat vehicles joined in the gas attack. Soon, Mount Carmel's main building was filled with gas, debris, and dust. But the gas masks protected most of the Davidians from the effects of the gas.

At 12:07 P.M., just a few minutes after the start of the gas attack, a Branch Davidian named Ruth Riddle ran from the compound. In her jacket was a computer disk containing David

Smoke billows from the Branch Davidian compound on April 19, 1993, as the shootout between ATF agents and cult members comes to a close.

Koresh's finished manuscript on Revelation. At the same moment, witnesses noticed plumes of smoke rising from several spots inside Mount Carmel. Soon, flames appeared. It was a windy day, and the blaze spread quickly through the wood-framed buildings. Eventually, the fire reached the Davidians' weapons storage area, causing loud explosions. Fire and rescue vehicles arrived, but not soon enough. Within half an hour, the compound was leveled. Later, when the smoke cleared, the world would learn that eighty-five Branch Davidians had died in the inferno, including twenty-five children and teens. Among the dead were most of David Koresh's children, several of his wives, and Koresh himself.

It is not clear what happened to spark the blaze inside Mount Carmel. It also may never be completely clear why dozens of Koresh's followers were willing to perish with him inside Mount Carmel rather than surrender. Part of the answer is that to the Davidians, Koresh represented an authority higher than human laws. As one scholar writes:

> Those at Mount Carmel believed that their eternal salvation depended upon their adherence to the message Koresh taught and, indeed, to Koresh himself as the bearer of that message. . . . As God's messiah, Koresh could actually intercede in their behalf and represent them sympathetically before God.[39]

Like so many other charismatic leaders, David Koresh was viewed by his followers as a direct line to God and a chance at salvation. For him, they were willing to sacrifice anything—even their own lives.

NOTES

Chapter 1: "Cults" and Their Leaders

1. Rebecca Moore, interview with the author, April 8, 1999.
2. J. Gordon Melton, *Encyclopedic Handbook of Cults in America*. New York: Garland, 1986, p. 5.
3. Anthony Storr, *Feet of Clay*. New York: Free Press, 1996, p. xiii.

Chapter 2: Mother Ann Lee: The Shakers

4. Nardi Reeder Campion, *Mother Ann Lee: Morning Star of the Shakers*. Hanover, NH: University Press of New England, 1990, p. 132.
5. Edward Deming Andrews, *The People Called Shakers*. New York: Oxford University Press, 1953, p. 8.
6. Campion, *Mother Ann Lee*, p. 21.
7. Quoted in Andrews, *The People Called Shakers*, p. 14.
8. Todd Burdick, interview with the author, April 7, 1999.
9. Quoted in Andrews, *The People Called Shakers*, p. 28.
10. Quoted in Campion, *Mother Ann Lee*, p. 94.
11. Campion, *Mother Ann Lee*, p. 136.

Chapter 3: Father Divine: The Universal Peace Mission Movement

12. Jill Watts, *God, Harlem, U.S.A.: The Father Divine Story*. Berkeley: University of California Press, 1992, p. 11.
13. Watts, *God, Harlem, U.S.A.*, p. 52.
14. Quoted in Melton, *Encyclopedic Handbook of Cults in America*, p. 94.
15. Melton, *Encyclopedic Handbook of Cults in America*, p. 94.

Chapter 4: L. Ron Hubbard: The Church of Scientology

16. Quoted in Russell Miller, *Bare-Faced Messiah*. New York: Henry Holt, 1987, p. 37.
17. Quoted in Miller, *Bare-Faced Messiah*, p. 145.
18. Quoted in William A. Henry, "Scientology's Combative Guru," *Time*, February 10, 1986.
19. L. Ron Hubbard, *Scientology: The Fundamentals of Thought*. Los Angeles: Bridge Publications, 1988, p. 137.
20. Quoted in Miller, *Bare-Faced Messiah*, p. 293.

Chapter 5: Sun Myung Moon: The Unification Church

21. Nansook Hong, *In the Shadow of the Moons*. Boston: Little, Brown, 1998, p. 11.

22. Christopher Edwards, *Crazy for God: The Nightmare of Cult Life*. Englewood Cliffs, NJ: Prentice-Hall, 1979, p. 119.

23. Quoted in Frederick Sontag, *Sun Myung Moon and the Unification Church*. Nashville, TN: Abingdon, 1977, p. 137.

24. Quoted in Sontag, *Sun Myung Moon and the Unification Church*, p. 130.

25. Sun Myung Moon, "True Family and World Peace." Speech delivered in New York City, June 11, 1998. www.unification.net/1998.

Chapter 6: Jim Jones: The Peoples Temple

26. Tim Reiterman with John Jacobs, *Raven*. New York: E. P. Dutton, 1982, p. 22.

27. Quoted in John R. Hall, *Gone from the Promised Land*. New Brunswick, NJ: Transaction Publishers, 1987, p. 42.

28. Reiterman with Jacobs, *Raven*, p. 94.

29. Quoted in Arts and Entertainment Network, *Investigative Reports: Jonestown* (television program), November 1998.

30. Quoted in Arts and Entertainment Network, *Investigative Reports: Jonestown*.

31. J. Gordon Melton, interview with the author, December 8, 1998.

32. Quoted in John Butterworth, *Cults and New Faiths*. Elgin, IL: David C. Cook, 1981, p. 37.

33. Quoted in Mary McCormick Maaga, *Hearing the Voices of Jonestown*. Syracuse, NY: Syracuse University Press, 1998, p. 162.

34. Quoted in Maaga, *Hearing the Voices of Jonestown*, p. 162.

Chapter 7: David Koresh: The Branch Davidians

35. Clifford L. Linedecker, *Massacre at Waco, Texas*. New York: St. Martin's Press, 1993, p. 82.

36. Quoted in James D. Tabor and Eugene Gallagher, *Why Waco? Cults and the Battle for Religious Freedom in America*. Berkeley: University of California Press, 1995, p. 62.

37. Ivan Solotaroff, "The Last Revelation from Waco," *Esquire*, July 1993, p. 26.

38. Tabor and Gallagher, *Why Waco?*, p. 18.

39. Tabor and Gallagher, *Why Waco?*, p. 32.

For Further Reading

Joan D. Barghusen, *Cults*. San Diego, CA: Lucent Books, 1998. This overview describes the nature and history of cults, the different aspects of living in them, and the difficulty of leaving a cult.

Nancy O'Keefe Bolick and Sallie G. Randolph, *Shaker Villages*. New York: Walker, 1993. This book, aimed at readers in grades 5 and up, examines Shaker customs and beliefs during and after the leadership of Mother Ann Lee.

Daniel Cohen, *Cults*. Brookfield, CT: Millbrook Press, 1994. Seventh- to tenth-graders will find Cohen's concise history of cults valuable. Cohen is careful to point out the difficulty in deciding which groups deserve to be called cults.

Kay Marie Porterfield, *Straight Talk About Cults*. New York: Facts On File, 1995. Appropriate for middle-schoolers and above, this book describes some shared characteristics of cults and offers a brief history of the phenomenon.

Thomas Streissguth, *Charismatic Cult Leaders*. Minneapolis: Oliver Press, 1995. Well-written, easy-to-read profiles of eight famous cult leaders, from Mormon prophet Joseph Smith to David Koresh.

Karen Zeinert, *Cults*. Springfield, NJ: Enslow Publishers, 1997. A balanced overview of cults and cult leaders suitable for students in middle school and up.

WORKS CONSULTED

Books

Edward Deming Andrews, *The Gift to Be Simple*. New York: J. J. Augustin Publishers, 1940. A collection of Shaker hymns and prayers, with an informative introduction about the Shakers and Mother Ann Lee.

————, *The People Called Shakers*. New York: Oxford University Press, 1953. A comprehensive history of the Shaker movement and its leader, Mother Ann Lee.

John Butterworth, *Cults and New Faiths*. Elgin, IL: David C. Cook, 1981. Butterworth provides summaries of major cult groups of the 1960s and 1970s, describing key beliefs and practices.

Nardi Reeder Campion, *Mother Ann Lee: Morning Star of the Shakers*. Hanover, NH: University Press of New England, 1990. This well-written, detailed account of Ann Lee's life and work includes documented quotations from Lee's contemporaries that bring the Shakers to life.

Bent Corydon and L. Ron Hubbard Jr., *L. Ron Hubbard: Messiah or Madman?* Secaucus, NJ: Lyle Stuart, 1987. This unauthorized biography of Hubbard is based partially on the experiences and memories of his son, Ron Jr., who worked in the Church of Scientology for ten years before breaking away.

Christopher Edwards, *Crazy for God: The Nightmare of Cult Life*. Englewood Cliffs, NJ: Prentice-Hall, 1979. A former "Moonie" tells how he came to join the Unification Church and describes the beliefs and practices of this cult.

John R. Hall, *Gone from the Promised Land*. New Brunswick, NJ: Transaction Publishers, 1987. This well-written survey of the history of Jim Jones's Peoples Temple includes some biographical information on Jones.

Friends of L. Ron Hubbard, *L. Ron Hubbard: The Humanitarian*. Los Angeles: The L. Ron Hubbard Library, 1995. Hubbard's followers discuss how they believe their leader had a positive impact on society.

Nansook Hong, *In the Shadow of the Moons*. Boston: Little, Brown, 1998. A former daughter-in-law of the Reverend Sun Myung Moon tells about this leader's life and about her own experiences inside his family and church.

L. Ron Hubbard, *Scientology: The Fundamentals of Thought*. Los Angeles: Bridge Publications, 1988. Originally written in 1956, this best-selling book serves as a broad introduction to Scientology.

Clifford L. Linedecker, *Massacre at Waco, Texas*. New York: St. Martin's Press, 1993. A journalist offers a dramatic account of David Koresh's life and leadership of the Branch Davidians, ending with a lengthy description of the conflict in which more than eighty people died.

Mary McCormick Maaga, *Hearing the Voices of Jonestown*. Syracuse, NY: Syracuse University Press, 1998. An eloquently told story of the people at Jonestown, with emphasis on the ways issues of gender, race, and class came into play at the commune.

Karl Marx and Friedrich Engels, *The Communist Manifesto*. London: Penguin Books, 1967. This primary source, first published in German in 1848, introduces the concepts of socialism and may be helpful in understanding certain aspects of Jim Jones's thought.

J. Gordon Melton, *Encyclopedic Handbook of Cults in America*. New York: Garland, 1986. A world-renowned expert on religious movements offers a scholarly guide to some of the most prominent cults in this country. Includes extensive information on Father Divine, L. Ron Hubbard, Sun Myung Moon, and Jim Jones.

Russell Miller, *Bare-Faced Messiah*. New York: Henry Holt, 1987. Miller paints a detailed portrait of L. Ron Hubbard's life, emphasizing how the story available from public documents differs from the story taught by the Church of Scientology.

Shiva Naipaul, *Journey to Nowhere: A New World Tragedy*. New York: Simon & Schuster, 1980. Naipaul details the evolution of the Jonestown settlement based on interviews with former Peoples Temple members.

Tim Reiterman with John Jacobs, *Raven*. New York: E. P. Dutton, 1982. An in-depth biography of Peoples Temple leader Jim Jones written by a former *San Francisco Examiner* reporter who visited Jonestown in 1978 and was wounded by gunfire during the confrontation at the Port Kaituma airstrip.

Margaret Thaler Singer with Janja Lalich, *Cults in Our Midst*. San Francisco: Jossey-Bass, 1995. Singer focuses on the threat of cults to individuals and society. Her book is based on interviews with thousands of former cult members.

Frederick Sontag, *Sun Myung Moon and the Unification Church*. Nashville, TN: Abingdon, 1977. Sontag's book includes extensive quotations from members and former members of the church, plus a rare interview with Sun Myung Moon himself. Especially useful is Sontag's segment-by-segment explanation of *The Divine Principle.*

Anthony Storr, *Feet of Clay.* New York: Free Press, 1996. Storr, a clinical psychiatrist and professor, outlines the similarities among gurus, or charismatic spiritual leaders, including such well-known cult leaders as Jim Jones, David Koresh, and Sun Myung Moon.

James D. Tabor and Eugene Gallagher, *Why Waco? Cults and the Battle for Religious Freedom in America.* Berkeley: University of California Press, 1995. These authors approach the story of David Koresh and the Branch Davidians from the perspective of religious scholars. They explain the role Koresh's beliefs played in the deadly standoff and argue that if government officials had paid closer attention to those teachings, the tragedy at Waco could have been prevented.

Jill Watts, *God, Harlem, U.S.A.: The Father Divine Story.* Berkeley: University of California Press, 1992. This biographer relies on exhaustive research to provide an in-depth, balanced picture of Father Divine's life, theology, and social programs.

Internet Sources

The Church of Scientology. The official website of the group founded by L. Ron Hubbard. It includes some biographical information about Hubbard. www.scientology.org

Sun Myung Moon, "True Family and World Peace." Transcript of speech delivered in New York City, June 11, 1998. www.unification.net/1998.

Periodicals

William A. Henry, "Scientology's Combative Guru," *Time,* February 10, 1986.

Peter Maas, "Moonskies," *New Republic,* November 9, 1990.

Eugene Methvin, "Scientology: Anatomy of a Frightening Cult," *Reader's Digest,* May 1980.

Anson Shupe, "Sun Myung Moon's American Disappointment," *Christian Century,* August 22, 1990.

Ivan Solotaroff, "The Last Revelation from Waco," *Esquire,* July 1993.

Interviews

Todd Burdick, author interview. April 7, 1999. Burdick is the director of education at Hancock Shaker Village in Hancock, Massachusetts.

Mary Maaga, author interview. December 2, 1998. Maaga is a religious scholar who has researched and written extensively about Jonestown and the Peoples Temple.

J. Gordon Melton, author interview. December 8, 1998. Melton is a leading expert on new religious movements.

Rebecca Moore, author interview. April 8, 1999. Moore, a professor of religious studies at the University of North Dakota, is the sister of two Peoples Temple members who died at Jonestown.

Catherine Wessinger, author interview. December 17, 1998. Wessinger is a professor of religious studies at Loyola University in New Orleans.

Video

Arts and Entertainment Network, *Investigative Reports: Jonestown.* First aired November 1998.

INDEX

PICTURE CREDITS

ABOUT THE AUTHOR

Karen Burns Kellaher has published several books for teachers and is the former editor of *Scholastic News*, a national current events weekly for children. She has published numerous nonfiction articles for students in grades 1–12. She holds a master of arts degree in publishing and education from the Gallatin School of New York University. Ms. Kellaher lives in New Jersey.